Reference Skills for the School Library Media Specialist: Tools and Tips

Second Edition

Ann Marlow Riedling

Professional Development Resources for K-12
Library Media and Technology Specialists

Library of Congress Cataloging-in-Publication Data

Riedling, Ann Marlow, 1952-
 Reference skills for the school library media specialist: tools and tips
/Ann Marlow Riedling.— 2nd ed.
 p. cm.
 Includes bibliographical references and indexes.
 ISBN 1-58683-190-9 (pbk.)
 1. School libraries—Reference services—United States. 2. Instructional
materials centers—United States. I. Title.

Z675.S3 R54 2005
025.5'2778—dc22

                           2004025097

Author: **Ann Marlow Riedling**

Linworth Books:
Carol Simpson, Editorial Director
Judi Repman, Associate Editor

Published by Linworth Publishing, Inc.
480 East Wilson Bridge Road, Suite L
Worthington, Ohio 43085

ISBN: 1-58683-190-9

5 4 3 2 1

Table of Contents

Table of Figures

Acknowledgments

Reference Skills for the School Library Media Specialist: Tools and Tips, Second Edition has been one of the most exciting looks into the future that I have taken! I would like to thank Donna Miller and all of the anonymous editors for their support, advise, guidance, and insights into this new edition.

Most of all, I express my deepest gratitude to my family—my husband, daughter, father, and mother—my energy, hope, support, and encouragement. Without them this book would not have been possible.

To all of these people—and many others—I thank you.

Dedication

I dedicate this second edition to my father (1921-1999), a true believer of libraries and a man of knowledge, wisdom, and love.

Introduction

Reference Skills for the School Library Media Specialist: Tools and Tips, Second Edition is designed for courses that prepare college and university students studying for an undergraduate or graduate degree in school library media. The objectives of this textbook are to teach basic reference processes, sources, services, and skills, and to provide authentic school library media reference scenarios and exercises for the purposes of reflection and guided application in today's reference world.

Few textbooks have been written concerning reference sources and services that are geared specifically and appropriately for the school library media specialist. With the ever-changing role of school library media specialists, the area of reference has also seen major alterations and adjustments, as well as the infusion of innovations; in particular, new technologies. The aim of this book is to address the current issues and concepts of reference resources and services with regard to the modern role of school library media specialists. This text includes references to the most recent American Association of School Librarians and Association for Educational Communications and Technology (AASL and AECT) guidelines, *Information Power: Building Partnerships for Learning*. School library media specialists should be influential in fostering effective and efficient access, evaluation, organization, and use of information. They are in a prime position to provide this information by instructing students to become information literate in the global society in which we live. This textbook serves as a practical manual with current basic reference information along with practical examples and exercises that provide prospective school library media specialists with insight into the numerous situations that arise in school library media centers.

Since the first edition of this textbook in 2000, school library media specialists and library media instructors have prodded me with comments such as, "We need your textbook updated to explain what we really need to know regarding reference services and skills, and to give us realistic and usable exercises, ones that we can refer to for specific situations in the school library media center." "We need to know where to turn for assistance regarding reference sources and services now that we are several years into the 21st century. Everything has changed so much."

The overall look of the second edition has not altered greatly. The chapter titles remain the same, with the exception of the last four chapters. Chapter 10 is altered because technology issues have been incorporated within the previous chapters—rather than separating them into a specific chapter. Chapter 10 is replaced with, The Web in Today's Reference Services, providing tips and tools for Internet reference use. The final chapter now includes one scenario and one reference example each—for elementary, middle, and high school situations.

To make an analogy, the trunk of reference has not changed (reference categories, basic reference interviewing skills, and so forth). However, the branches have exploded with new leaves and flowers—the result of innovative, time-saving, inspiring reference technologies. As a result, additional, up-to-date Web sites are included as well as scenarios and exercises that represent our world today. The second edition of this text introduces new reference resources (print, nonprint, and Web-based). Technology and reference sources and services change enormously within short time periods. To reflect these changes, all resources mentioned are current. All screen shots are up-to-date and functional (as of the writing of this book); all scenarios and exercises deal with today's school library reference dilemmas. In addition, an annotated Webliography has been added for many chapters, to make Web searching and reference services easier. Lastly, some chapters include "Useful Web sites," which supplement the material covered in the chapter.

Reference Skills for the School Library Media Specialist: Tools and Tips, Second Edition is divided into five parts:

Part I: What Is Reference All About? discusses reference processes, sources, and services, focusing on the human side of reference work. Significant school library media reference terminology, techniques, and concepts are addressed. Additionally, research processes and models such as the Big6 by Eisenberg and Berkowitz, Information Seeking by Kuhlthau, and the Research Process by Stripling and Pitts are outlined. Selection, evaluation, and maintenance of the reference collection are also discussed in Part I—methods and sources of discovering the appropriate print and electronic reference materials for the school library media situation, as well as effective organization of the collection.

Part II: Nuts and Bolts speaks about the actual types of reference sources used in modern school library media centers, including bibliographies, directories, almanacs, yearbooks, handbooks, biographical sources, dictionaries, encyclopedias, geographical sources, indexes, and abstracts. Print and electronic sources are not addressed separately, but occur together throughout the chapters, as electronic resources are prevalent in today's reference world.

Part III: The Art of Questioning focuses on the reference interview. This valuable conversation between the student and the school library media specialist connects knowledge with information needs. Proper and effective communication is a critical component of school library media reference services.

Part IV: Reference and the Web discusses our evolving world and the incredible growth of knowledge, explosion of technology, and speedy reconfiguration of the boundaries that separate the myriad of academic fields and social conventions. Collectively, and with the use of technologies that have augmented this momentum of change, humanity generates enormous amounts of information. The abilities to access, comprehend, use, and evaluate information are the skills students must develop in order to function in our current world. Part IV specifically addresses Web use with regard to reference sources and services.

Part V: Scenarios and Exercises consists of practical scenarios and useful exercises—a look into the real world of school library media reference services. This chapter is divided into elementary, middle, and high school level examples. The situations and examples include both practical and philosophical aspects of reference services and sources for school library media specialists. These are meant to be read thoughtfully, pondered, and hopefully discussed with other prospective or experienced school library media specialists. Following each situation or exercise is a list of questions included for consideration and reflection. Expectantly, attentive conversations by students will arise from the readings through guided instruction; discussions that will search the very heart of reference services for school library media specialists.

PART 1

What is Reference All About?

Chapter *1*

Reference and the School Library: An Overview

Introduction

It is said that there exists a university library in the United States that has carved over its front entrance, "The half of knowledge is knowing where to find it." I would like to add the following words: evaluate, organize, and use of information. School library media reference services, in the past, as now, assist students to get a better value from the library media collection than they would have on their own. Reference for school library media specialists is more than a skilled technique. It is a profoundly human activity ministering to one of the most basic needs of humans—the desire to know. Reference processes, sources, and services revolve around the basic principle of maximization of resources, which underlies all reference work.

Reference Services

What the school library media specialist does with regard to reference services is fundamentally to answer questions. The school library media specialist must have the ability to then translate questions into terms that can be understood by aligning them with proper resources. This is known as reference services. As explained by Kenneth Whittaker, "The purpose of reference and information service is to align information to flow efficiently from information sources to those who need it. Without the [school library media specialist] bringing source and [student] together, the flow would either never take place at all or only take place inefficiently" (49). As a school library media specialist, you act as a mediator between the perplexed student and too much, or too little, information. As a mediator, the school library media specialist weighs the good, the bad, and the indifferent data to locate accurate sources to meet the information needs of students. The school library media specialist assists the students in determining what they need out of the ever-growing masses of print and electronic information.

Successful reference services for school library media specialists consist of three components: 1) knowledge of the library media collection; 2) effective conversational skills (communication); and 3) competence in selecting, acquiring, and evaluating resources to meet students' needs. Corresponding with these three components are two basic functions of library media center services: 1) the provision of information; and 2) instruction or guidance in the use of information sources. The American Library Association explains that library media centers exist for the purpose of information and enlightenment. They are institutions with an educational [instruction] and informational [provision of information] purpose.

The accurate and appropriate provision of information will occur when the school library media specialist has a complete and accurate knowledge of the library media center collection, along with competence in selecting, acquiring, and evaluating that collection. School library media collections consist of a variety of resources; what is a resource? A resource is any source or material, regardless of form or location, which provides necessary answer(s). According to *Information Power*'s *Learning and Teaching Principles*, the library media center should provide, "…access to the full range of information resources…" (AASL and AECT 58). It further states that the library media center should, "…offer a full range of instructional and informational resources that all students need to meet their curriculum goals" (AASL and AECT 90). (Proper selection and evaluation processes and techniques are discussed in the following chapter.)

Instruction or guidance in the use of information sources by the school library media specialist is dependent upon effective conversational (communication) skills. It has been suggested that the library media center is an agency of communication. Guidance is vitally important! The school library media specialist should never lose sight of the fact that, to the student, the question is only partly a technical requirement; at a deeper level that information is required to satisfy a basic cognitive need. (Effective communication and conversational skills and techniques are addressed in more detail in chapter nine.)

Instruction or guidance reference services teach or direct students to locate information themselves. It provides them with an understanding of reference tools and techniques, their correct usage, and how the library media center and information are organized. Instructional services also advise and assist students in the identification and selection of appropriate materials about a given topic. Instruction or guidance may occur with individuals or groups; however, the end result remains the same—educating students regarding access, evaluation, organization, and use of reference sources and services. It is important to remain aware of the fact that school library media specialists lead students to information (many times on their own), not knowledge. Students manipulate the information and construct knowledge from that information.

School library media specialists often provide orientations to inform students as to the organization and scope of the library media center's resources. This is a significant aspect of reference services for school library media specialists. Additionally, orientations are many times employed as a means of welcoming students and encouraging visitation to the library media center.

Reference instruction is also termed bibliographic instruction. Bibliographic instruction is an expression widely used and accepted in the modern library world. It is defined as any activity that is designed to teach students how to locate and use information, which goes beyond the physical boundaries of the school library media center. With the explosion of technologies that exist within, and yet beyond the walls of library media centers today, the term bibliographic instruction more accurately defines what school library media specialists do with regard to reference work and the education of today's students—teaching lifelong learning skills.

The Reference Process

The day of seeking answers has not ended; only the process has changed. What is the reference process? Fundamentally, it consists of the entire transaction with the student in the course of which the reference work is carried out. Basically, it contains three primary elements: 1) information; 2) student; and 3) answer. These elements combine with five specific steps to create the complete reference process: 1) a need for information; 2) a question; 3) the search for information; 4) an answer or response; and 5) an evaluation. (Figure 1.1 on page 6 more thoroughly explains these five steps in the reference process.) The reference process may be simply explained as problem solving. It is the solution of the student's problem that is the real object of the process. As fixed as this process may appear, school library media specialists must keep in mind that each question is unique; therefore, each process will be unique as well. The reference process is merely an outline; what occurs within the text differs from situation to situation, student to student.

Figure 1.1: The Reference Process: Five Basic Steps

The Reference Process: Five Basic Steps

1. A Need for Information
   A request is made.
2. A Question
   What problem needs solving? What decision or choice needs making? What data and insight are required to shed light on the main question? What are the smaller questions that will help create an answer to the primary question? What does the student already know? What is missing? What does the student not know?
3. The Search for Information
   Based on the question(s), the student and school library media specialist develop research problem-solving strategies. Where might the best information lie? What sources are likely to provide the most insight with the most efficiency? Which resources are reliable? What steps will be required to protect against bias and develop a balanced view? Which sources are the most current?
   Location and identification of resources occurs.
4. An Answer or Response
   Information is sorted and organized; synthesis should occur.
   Are different resources required? Are additional resources required? Is the information provided complete? Does the student understand the information? Is the student information literate—learned how to learn?
5. An Evaluation
   Has the need(s) been met? Was the reference process complete or incomplete?

Reference and Information Literacy

In the technological, global society of today, information literacy cannot be overlooked. The essential philosophy surrounding school reference service is the encouragement of lifelong learning—or information literacy. The American Library Association describes information literate individuals as "…people who have learned how to learn. They know how to learn because they know how knowledge is organized, how to find information…They are people prepared for lifelong learning" (AASL and AECT 7). The abilities to access, comprehend, use, and evaluate information have become the skills people must develop in order to function in our current world. *Information Power*'s *Information Literacy Standards for Student Learning* explicitly outline what students should possess in order to be information literate in today's society, "…accesses information efficiently and effectively…evaluates information critically and competently…uses information accurately and creatively…" (AASL and AECT 8). (Figure 1.2 on page 7 more completely explains the information literacy process as it relates to student learning.) School library media reference services play a particularly important role in fostering information literacy through the provision of information, instruction and direction.

Figure 1.2: The Information Literacy Process as It Relates to Student Learning

The Information Literacy Process

At the onset of the information literacy process, the student will:

Identify a Need or Problem

> Be inquisitive about a wide range of topics, issues and problems.
> Recognize the need for accurate and complete information.
> Brainstorm to focus the topic and formulate research questions.

Once the topic is focused and the questions formulated, the student will:

Seek Appropriate Resources

> Identify potential sources of information (print, electronic, community, etc.)
> Utilize effective research problem-solving strategies.
> Evaluate sources for appropriateness (reading level, biases, etc.)

After the resources have been identified and evaluated, the student will:

Gather Information

> Read, view, and hear a wide variety of appropriate materials.
> Gain background knowledge about the topic.
> Begin to build in-depth knowledge regarding certain aspects of the topic.

As the material is being read, viewed, and heard, the student will:

Analyze Information

> Skim and scan for keywords and major ideas.
> Determine the accuracy, relevance, and reliability of the information.
> Differentiate between fact and opinion, agreement, disagreement, etc.
> Identify biases, points of view, and cultural diversity.

After analyzing the information, the student will:

Interpret and Synthesize Information

> Summarize and paraphrase the information.
> Draw conclusions based on collected information.
> Create new information to replace inaccurate, misleading information as required.
> Integrate new information with prior knowledge.
> Logically organize and sequence the information.
> Apply information into critical thinking and problem solving to complete the task.

Following the summarization of the information, the student will:

Communicate Information

> Select a presentation format appropriate for the purpose and audience.
> Document sources using an appropriate format.

To properly assess the learning process and identify areas needing further development and practice, the student will:

Evaluate Process and Product

> Conduct an on-going evaluation by revising, improving, and updating the process and product as required.
> Determine if the project or process met the defined need(s).
> Determine what new skills/knowledge was gained.

Research Problem-Solving Processes and Models

Our complex, global society continues to expand at a rate beyond the capacity of individuals to comprehend. Access, evaluation, organization, and use of information are critical to ease the burden of change and to assist humanity in navigating its course towards the future. It is imperative that students possess the skills required to learn efficiently and effectively. By discussing research problem-solving strategies explicitly, it is more likely that these processes will be transferred to future research problem-solving situations.

Figure 1.3: Overview of Three Research or Problem-Solving Models or Processes: Information Seeking, Big6 Information Problem-Solving, Research Process

Overview of Three Research or Problem-Solving Models or Processes

Information Seeking	Big6 Information Problem Solving	Research Process
Kuhlthau	**Eisenberg and Berkowitz**	**Stripling and Pitts**
Task initiation	Task identification	Choose broad topic
Topic selection		Overview of topic
		Narrow the topic
Formulation of focus	Information seeking strategies	Develop purpose
Exploration		Formulate question
		Plan for research
Collection	Location and access	Analyze, evaluate
	Information use	Evaluate evidence
Presentation	Synthesis	Make conclusions
Assessment	Evaluation	Create, present
		Reflection

The following three processes or models are widely accepted and used as problem-solving strategies in schools: Information Seeking by Carol Kuhlthau, the Big6 Information Problem-Solving Model by Michael Eisenberg and Robert Berkowitz, and the Research Process by Barbara Stripling and Judy Pitts. (Figure 1.3 on this page provides a brief overview of these three models.)

Carol Kuhlthau's six-stage model of the Information Seeking process conceptualizes the construction of meaning through active participation with information resources. This model encourages an in-depth focus that enables students to seek more relevant information and produce a product of higher quality. Kuhlthau states, "Living in the information age requires people to go beyond the ability to locate information and requires competence in seeking meaning and understanding. More is not necessarily better without skillful guidance from an insightful person [school library media specialist]" (*Learning* 708). (Figure 1.4 on this page displays this process as it relates to affective, cognitive, and sensorimotor learning.)

Figure 1.4: Carol Kuhlthau's Information Seeking Process: Affective, Cognitive, Sensorimotor Learning

The Information Seeking Process: Affective, Cognitive, and Sensorimotor Learning

STAGE	Affective	Cognitive	Sensorimotor
Task Initiation	Uncertainty	General; Vague Thoughts	Recognizing one's information need
Topic Selection	Optimism	Scheduling or Planning	Identifying one's search problem
Exploration	Confusion; Frustration	Being informed about topic	Investigating scope of topic
Formulation	Ease accompanying clarity	Narrowing of topic focus	Formulating a search question
Collection	Sense of direction & confidence	Defining, supporting focus	Gathering notes
Presentation	Satisfied or Dissatisfied	More focused comprehension	Completing a report

One recent, well-known information problem-solving model is the Big6 approach by Michael Eisenberg and Robert Berkowitz. This process describes the six thinking steps one goes through any time there is an information problem to be solved. Eisenberg explains it this way, "'Brainstorm and narrow' is the essential process for information seeking strategies…[students should] brainstorm all possible information sources to meet the task, and then critically determine the best sources for completing the particular task" (22). (An overview of the Big6 problem-solving model is displayed in Figure 1.5 on page 10.)

The Big6 Information Problem-Solving Model

Task Definition
Define the problem.
Identify the information.
These questions should be asked prior to beginning the search:
What type of information do you need to solve your problem? Do you need current or historical materials? Do you need many or few sources?

Information Seeking Strategies
Determine the range of possible resources.
Evaluate the different possible sources to determine priorities.
Determine what sources of information are available.
Be cognizant of the need to tailor the amount of information to meet specific needs.

Location and Access
Locate sources.
Find information within sources.

Use of Information
Engage.
Extract relevant information (requires the majority of time).
Note sources used; produce accurate citations.

Synthesis
Organize information from multiple sources.
Present information in an appropriate format.

Evaluation
Judge the process or product.

The *Research Process* developed by Barbara Stripling and Judy Pitts connects information handling and use with subject matter that is essential for learning to occur. Stripling and Pitts discovered that students have little prior knowledge of the information-seeking process, have fragmented understandings of subject knowledge, and that students do not understand that their information seeking knowledge depends on content knowledge and vice versa. As a result, school library media specialists should plan instruction to specifically assist students in attaining these skills. Learning experiences should be viewed holistically, recognizing that one area (i.e., information search process) can support other areas (i.e., content knowledge) and so forth. As Pitts noted, "There are many different, acceptable paths to the same end. Every…[student seemed] to have a different approach to working on a research assignment and organizing information. Each system worked well, but if everyone had been ordered to use one specific approach many students would have found themselves incredibly frustrated" (23).

As explained in *Information Power: Building Partnerships for Learning*, "Information literacy—the ability to find and use information—is the keystone to lifelong learning. Creating a foundation for lifelong learning is at the heart of the school library media program….The school library media specialist can use the information literacy standards for student learning to create and maintain a program for a broad learning community—students, teachers, administrators, parents, and the neighborhood—that will support lifelong learning" (AASL and AECT 1).

The Nine Information Literacy Standards for Student Learning

Taken from *Information Power: Building Partnerships for Learning* (AASL and ACET 8).

INFORMATION LITERACY

Standard 1: The student who is information literate accesses information efficiently and effectively.

Standard 2: The student who is information literate evaluates information critically and competently.

Standard 3: The student who is information literate uses information accurately and creatively.

INDEPENDENT LEARNING

Standard 4: The student who is an independent learner is information literate and pursues information related to personal interests.

Standard 5: The student who is an independent learner is information literate and appreciates literature and other creative expressions of information.

Standard 6: The student who is an independent learner is information literate and strives for excellence in information seeking and knowledge generation.

SOCIAL RESPONSIBILITY

Standard 7: The student who contributes positively to the learning community and to society is information literate and recognizes the importance of information to a democratic society.

Standard 8: The student who contributes positively to the learning community and to society is information literate and practices ethical behavior in regard to information and information technology.

Standard 9: The student who contributes positively to the learning community and to society is information literate and participates effectively in groups to pursue and generate information.

Numerous additional information problem-solving research models and processes have been developed and can be extremely valuable and useful in developing school library media reference services. Information problem-solving and critical thinking involve the application, analysis, synthesis, and evaluation of information to construct personal meaning. Without this ability, students cannot go beyond the mere collection of information in order to weave information threads together into the creation of knowledge. Our role as school library media specialists is to encourage the appropriate problem-solving research processes, as well as critical thinking, in order to lead students to information. Ultimately self-directed learners lead themselves to knowledge from that information.

Reference and the Technology Connection

Less than two decades ago information sources were synonymous with print materials. It is now an anomaly to use only printed resources in the realm of reference work. Although reference services are changing in dynamic ways for school library media specialists, their essence—the provision of assistance to students seeking information—remains stable. The process of reference services is changing; the goal (the answer) remains constant. Technologies have made it possible to reach that goal faster and with more efficiency. The rapid growth and availability of information in electronic form is transforming the entire role of the school library media specialist and reference services as well. It has created a whole new range of options for finding and delivering information desired by students. With all the technologies available in our current, global world, why are reference services still needed? They are required to determine, among the tons of information, the ounce necessary and useful for the student. They are required to assist students in learning how to access, organize, evaluate, and use information—learn how to learn, become information literate. Ironically, technology has actually increased the student's need for assistance and reference services. With this in mind, school library media specialists face an opportunity and challenge—not an easy, but a necessary one—in response to the technological, societal changes of our modern times.

Conclusion

The three elements necessary for the reference process are the information/direction, the student, and the answer. One critical element concerning reference sources and services in today's technological society is information literacy. School library media specialists should foster information literacy, defined as the ability to access, comprehend, use, and evaluate information. School library media specialists must help students learn how to learn, to become lifelong learners. Reference work for the school library media specialist is a diverse variety of activities that can be viewed under the two headings of: provision of information, and instruction or direction. What the school library media specialist does with regard to reference work is to answer questions, to assist in leading students to information. In order to efficiently and effectively conduct reference services, the media specialist should possess three things: knowledge of the collection, effective communication skills, and competence in selecting, organizing, and evaluating resources. The reference process consists of five basic steps that should be used as a guideline when conducting reference services: a need for information, a question, a search for information, an answer or response, and an evaluation.

Reference sources and services are constantly changing in response to new societal and technological developments in our information-hungry society. There exists an increased importance and availability of information. There is no doubt that expanding electronic applications will continue to contribute to the importance of reference services. It is argued that new electronic resources will also lead to an expansion of the guidance and instructional role of school library media specialists in the years ahead. School library media centers and reference services are intended to enrich society and contribute to students' efforts to learn. The challenge is ours.

Useful Web Sites

Information Inquiry for Teachers
> http://eduscapes.com/info/pitts.html
> *The REACTS Taxonomy (Recalling, Explaining, Analyzing, Challenging, Transforming, Synthesizing), developed by Barbara Stripling and Judy Pitts, focuses on critical thinking in the research process.*

Information Inquiry for Teachers
> http://eduscapes.com/info/big6.html
> *This Web site provides in-depth information regarding the Big6 and Super3, created by Michael Eisenberg and Robert Berkowitz.*

Information Power
> http://www.ala.org/ala/aasl/aaslproftools/informationpower/informationpower.htm
> *This site offers a wealth of information regarding* Information Power: Building Partnerships for Learning, *as well as the American Association of School Libraries (AASL).*

KidsSpace @ The Internet Public Library
> http://www.ipl.org/div/kidspace/browse/ref8000/
> *This site provides numerous links that can be helpful for all types of homework—math, science, English, and more.*

Kuhlthau's Information Search Process
> http://www.scils.rutgers.edu/~kuhlthau/Search%20Process.htm
> *This site provides a wonderful overview of the Information Search Process, including a PowerPoint presentation by Carol Kuhlthau.*

Library Spot
> http://www.libraryspot.com/
> *This Web site offers encyclopedias, maps, online libraries, quotations, associations, children's services, and much more.*

Online Resources for School Library Media Specialists: Web Gateways to Information
> http://www.school-libraries.org/resources/gateways.html
> *Via this site, online resources are selected and made available, as a way of assisting school library media specialists to make effective use of the vast resources of the Internet and World Wide Web.*

Ready, Set Go! Reference Sources on the Web
> http://www.infotoday.com/MMSchools/jan97mms/cybee197.htm
> *This Web site offers school library media specialists with some welcome relief—searching the Web far and wide for the very best ready reference locations, such as encyclopedias, calendars, and so forth.*

Reference Resources
> http://www.newschool.edu/library/libraria.htm
> *This site includes "Best Free Reference Sources for 2002," from the American Library Association, including dictionaries, thesauri, telephone directories, Internet search engines, and much more.*

The School Librarian's Desktop Reference
> http://www.delanet.com/~ftise/liblinks.html
> *This Web site is arranged by subject and includes Web sites, listservs, and search tools, as well as links to acquisitions, automation, cataloging, and so on.*

Tutorial for Info Power
> http://tip.uwyo.edu/intro1.htm
> *This site offers a helpful tutorial regarding information literacy, using the premise of Investigate, Search, Locate, Evaluate, and Use.*

Chapter *2*

Selection, Evaluation, and Maintenance of the Reference Collection

Introduction

How does a school library media specialist know what reference materials are needed in the school library media center? How does he or she know if a reference resource is good, bad, or indifferent? Following the rule of a good reference source is one that serves to answer a question; the focus of this chapter is effective selection and evaluation of reference resources for school library media centers. In explaining the effective selection and evaluation of library media center reference materials, it is important to recall a principle in *Information Power*'s *Information Access and Delivery*, which states, "The collections of the [school library media center] are developed and evaluated collaboratively to support the school's curriculum and to meet the diverse learning needs of students" (AASL and AECT 90).

What is a reference source? It can be defined as materials, from book to computer to periodical to photograph, designed to be consulted for definite items of information rather than to be examined consecutively. Reference sources can be divided into two main classes: 1) compilations that furnish information directly (encyclopedias, dictionaries, almanacs, handbooks, yearbooks, biographical sources, directories, atlases); and 2) compilations that refer to other sources containing information, merely indicating places in which information can be found (bibliographies and indexes). Adequate and appropriate selection and evaluation of reference materials involves consideration of specific criteria and aids or tools that may be useful in collection development. (Both types of reference sources are explained in detail in the following chapters.) School library media specialists have a multitude of tasks; one critical task is the selection and evaluation of reference materials—print and electronic. Without the proper tools, expertise or good judgment to accomplish this task, students' informational needs may remain unanswered.

What Do You Need?—The Selection Process

Selection is the process of deciding what materials to add to the school library media collection. In choosing reference resources, a school library media specialist plans and carries out certain activities that culminate in selection decisions. These activities include identifying and assessing evaluative information about reference materials, examining the resources, and providing ways to involve others in the selection process. Meeting curriculum needs is a major criterion for placing items in the media center collection. School library media specialists should review on a regular basis textbooks used by all teachers, assess teachers' instructional methods, and become aware of particular research and other assignments given by teachers. One of the most important tasks of a school library media specialist is to help students and teachers find the best materials available—in all formats—to support teaching and learning.

All materials, including reference, should meet the criteria of the library media center selection policy. Selection policies are vital because they explain the process followed and the priorities established before any resource is purchased and placed in the school library collection. A selection policy will state the selection aids used in choosing resources. Numerous tools or aids review new reference publications. Remember, however, that selection is not completely the responsibility of the school library media specialist. It also belongs to administrators, teachers, students, parents, and community members. Input from these people is essential for a useful and appropriate reference collection.

A number of tools or aids are available to assist the school library media specialist in deciding which resources are needed for possible inclusion in the reference collection. Reviews are critical to suitable selection and evaluation of reference materials. However, the school library media specialist's informed judgment in the selection of materials best suited to the library media center and student population is of equal importance. Regardless of the situation, a thorough knowledge of the library media center's existing resources is imperative. There are numerous journals, guidebooks, and online sources to assist school library media specialists with the selection of print and electronic reference materials. Most journals contain reviews of electronic media as well as print sources; articles, columns, editorials, and other information are also included. The following are examples of effective selection tools or aids:

All grade levels:

- *American Libraries* (American Library Association)
  American Libraries magazine, available in both print and online formats lists outstanding reference sources for small and medium-sized libraries. The Reference and User Services Association's (RUSA) Reference Sources Committee lists the best reference materials of the year online; this list is available with annotations in the May issue of the print version of *American Libraries*.

- *American Reference Books Annual* (Libraries Unlimited, Inc.)
  American Reference Books Annual has been published annually since 1970 and is currently available in print format, including annotations, reviews, and other commentary useful for selection and evaluation of reference materials for school library media specialists. It is now available online at: http://lu.com._

- *Booklist* (American Library Association)
  The American Library Association publishes this journal semimonthly, 22 times per year. *Booklist* includes Reference Books Bulletin, which focuses specifically on reference resources for the school media center. It reviews current books, videos, and software and provides monthly author/title indexes as well as semiannual cumulative indexes.

- *The Horn Book Magazine* (The Horn Book, Inc.)
  The Horn Book Magazine examines children's resources, including reference materials; and they also publish reviews, articles, editorials, columns, and so forth. *Horn Book* is published six times per year and reviews hardback and paperback books. *Horn Book* includes bibliographic information, size, age level, summary of content, and other pertinent information regarding the selection of elementary materials.

- *Library Media Connection* (Linworth Publishing, Inc.)
  Library Media Connection is a magazine, newly revised, that includes their two previous magazines, *Library Talk* and *The Book Report*. It provides integrated information for print and multimedia materials, innovative ideas, and practical tips and techniques (appropriate for all age levels). This inclusive magazine includes reviews of books, software, and CD-ROMs, written by professionals in the school library media field.

- *MultiMedia & Internet@Schools* (Information Technology, Inc.)
  http://www.infotoday.com/MMSchools/default.shtml
  MultiMedia & Internet@Schools is available in print and online formats. It provides reviews of books, CD-ROMs, databases and online sources, hardware, and other technologies appropriate for K-12 school library media centers.

- *School Library Journal* (R. R. Bowker Co.)
  School Library Journal (SLJ) is a leading magazine for school library media specialists. One half of SLJ is dedicated to critical reviews of print and electronic resources. SLJ provides 12 issues per year; the December copy presents the editor's choices for Best Books of the Year. SLJ now includes a "free trial zone," which allows school library media specialists to browse databases from publishers and vendors.

- *A Guide to Reference Materials for School Library Media Centers, 5th Edition*
  (Libraries Unlimited, Inc.)
  This print resource covers more than 2,000 titles and includes age and reading levels, presentation styles, strengths and weaknesses, comparisons with other titles, citations, and reviews.

Primary and elementary grade levels:
- *Children's Catalog* (H. W. Wilson)
  Children's Catalog (print format) provides a wide-ranging annotated listing of more than 6,000 of the best fiction and nonfiction books, new and established, written for children from preschool through sixth grade—print and online versions.
- *Reference Books for Children, 4th edition* (Scarecrow Press)
  Reference Books for Children (print format) evaluates reference works and selection tools in addition to discussing criteria for selecting such resources. Author, title, and subject indexes are provided.

Secondary grade levels:
- *Books for Young Adults, Grades Nine through Twelve* (Brodart)
  Books for Young Adults reviews more than 50,000 new and backlist titles. Titles are accessible by awards, starred reviews, publisher series, subject categories, and Dewey classification.
- *The Middle and Junior High School Library Catalog* (H. W. Wilson)
  The Middle and Junior High School Library Catalog (print and online formats), now in its 8th edition, includes grades five through eight. This catalog provides an annotated list of more than 4,000 fiction and nonfiction books published in the United States, Canada, and the United Kingdom.
- *The Senior High School Library Catalog, 16th Edition* (H. W. Wilson)
  The Senior High School Library Catalog (print and online formats) represents a well-balanced collection of more than 5,000 outstanding fiction and nonfiction titles essential to the senior high school library collection (grades nine through 12).

Online sources:
- KidsClick.com (www.KidsClick.com)
  KidsClick provides educational and fun software just for kids!
- Reference Center at the Internet Public Library (http://www.ipl.org/)
  The Reference Center at the Internet Public Library online resource includes links such as: Subject Collections, Ready Reference, Reading Rooms, KidSpace, TeenSpace, Special Collections, and much more.
- Reference Desk at Librarians' Index to the Internet (http://www.lii.org)
  Reference Desk at Librarians' Index to the Internet is a searchable, annotated subject directory of thousands of Internet resources including arts, education, government, science, sports, and so forth.

Additional tools may include selection sources published by the American

Library Association (http://www.ala.org), the Association for Educational Communications and Technology (http://www.aect.org), Gale Research (http://www.gale.com), H. W. Wilson (http://www.hwwilson.com), and R. R. Bowker (http://www.bowker.com). Reviews from professional journals in major academic areas should be considered as well. Reference selection tools or aids serve to assist the school library media specialist in evaluating sources for possible inclusion into the library media center, as well as identifying gaps in the reference collection. However, these are merely aids; they can only assist if the school library media specialist has a complete knowledge of the collection and uses good judgment based on the existing resources and the needs of the community and students served.

How Do You Know If It's Good?—The Evaluation Process

A good reference source is one that serves to answer questions and a bad reference source is one that fails to answer questions. Still another function as a school library media specialist is to continually evaluate the quality of the library media center's reference collection. By using appropriate evaluation tools and criteria, the school library media specialist is better able to judge whether a particular source meets the needs of the student population. While evaluation criteria were originally developed for printed sources, the evaluation of electronic information considers many of the same elements, with several added components. Much is subjective when judging any kind of resource. However, the following criteria (appropriate for both print and electronic information) will assist school library media specialists in evaluating reference resources of value to meet students' informational needs:

> **Content Scope**: Identifying the scope of material presented is the basic breadth and depth question of what is covered and in what detail. The scope should reflect the purpose of the source and its intended audience. Has the author or editor accomplished what was intended? How current are the contents? Aspects of scope include subject, geographical and time period coverage. Evaluating scope includes reviewing topical aspects of the subject about which the resource is focused and noting if there are any key omissions from the subject area. For printed materials, the statement of purpose is generally found in the preface, introduction or contents; for an electronic site, one should look for the stated purpose on the site, along with any limitations that may apply, and site comprehensiveness. Information about CD-ROMs and DVDs can usually be found in the publisher or vendor's descriptive materials.

> **Accuracy, Authority, and Bias**: Indicators of authority include the education and experience of the authors, editors, and contributors, as well as the reputation of the publisher or sponsoring agency. Typically, it is easier to evaluate the authority of printed reference sources, because statements of authorship and lists of references can be more easily identified. On the other hand, it is at times extremely difficult to discover who actually provided the information on an electronic site. Some items to look for include who provided the information, why, and explicit

statements of authority. Objectivity and fairness of a source are also important considerations. Does the author or contributor have biases? How reliable are the facts presented? Many times this can be assessed by examining the coverage of controversial issues and the balance in coverage given to various subjects. Was the site developed as a means of advertisement or as scholarly material? The creator of the information may serve as an indicator of biases on electronic sites.

Arrangement and Presentation: Printed sources arrange entries in a particular sequence, such as alphabetical, chronological, or classified. If the sequence is familiar, the user may be able to directly find the information sought, rather than using an index. The flexibility of the reference source is typically enhanced by the availability of indexes offering different types of access to the information. Physical makeup, binding, illustrations, and layout are concerns with print resources. Presentation issues regarding electronic information include page or site layout, clarity or intuitiveness of the site's organizational design, and help or example sections. Some things to look for include appropriate audience, use of graphics, navigational links, and a table of contents.

Relation to Similar Works: A newly published material may have different types of relationships to sources already in your school library media center collection. These need to be taken into account in assessing the potential value of the new resource to the collection. What will this resource add to the current collection? Regarding electronic materials, it is important to assess the extent to which the content corresponds (time period covered, more information provided, etc.).

Timeliness and Permanence: Printed resources are often considered to be out of date before they reach the student. All sources should be checked for currency. Sometimes relevant information on an electronic site can be located in a document header or footer. Information to observe includes posting and revision dates, policy statements for information maintenance, and link maintenance. It is also significant to recognize that there is no guarantee that a particular file of information will reside in the same location today as it did yesterday. A good strategy is to note the date and time a site is visited if one intends to use the information and a citation is taken.

Cost: Sometimes budget, rather than student need, may determine whether a particular reference source is purchased. The cost of print materials and those in distributed electronic form are similar, in that a copy is acquired for in-house use in the school library media center, and the purchase or subscription price buys unlimited access to the contents of the resource. However, online costs may vary widely. In assessing the cost, the school library media specialist must attempt to determine if the price is appropriate in relation to the needs of the students, as well as anticipated frequency and length of use. Also, the school library media specialist must consider licenses for software and other related issues. In the case of electronic materials, it is important to consider the cost of hardware and maintenance as well.

Collection Organization and Maintenance

Accurate arrangement and maintenance of the reference collection is necessary in order to provide convenience and ease of use by the school library media specialist, as well as the student population. A reference collection that is unplanned or not weeded appropriately may prove ineffective and unresponsive to the information needs of students. A systematic basis for weeding, as well as adding new materials to the reference collection should exist. As a school library media specialist, what is already in the collection and what is actually needed for effective reference work by students must be taken into account. Factors affecting weeding of reference materials are similar to the total school library media center collection: age or currency of material, frequency of use, relevance, physical condition, format, and space availability. It is more important to have a small but relevant and up-to-date collection of materials than a large collection that is neither useful nor of good quality.

Some reference materials, obviously, become outdated. If so, a school library media specialist should consider the following basic guidelines: print encyclopedias should be replaced every five years (and the old ones not sent to a classroom, but discarded); pure science books, print format (except botany and natural history) are out of date within five years; any books dealing with technology should be replaced every five years (or more often); print information on inventions and medicine is dated within five years; print psychology, history, business, and education sources become dated in ten years; and newspapers and magazines, print format, should be kept up to five years (although most are now purchased either on CD-ROM or online). Where should these withdrawn materials go? If resources are weeded due to a change in curriculum, it may be beneficial to relocate them to another library. Otherwise, weeded materials should be destroyed. (Personally take them to a dumpster and throw them in!)

Current school library media center reference collections include sources in a variety of formats, from print materials to online sources. The school library media specialist must decide what format to purchase, as well as whether to obtain particular materials in more than one format. Although varying formats may overlap in content, they may differ in access capabilities. School library media specialists have more options than ever before in creating a reference collection that is adequate and appropriate for the school library, community, and students served.

Decisions in collection development include whether to buy new titles, to buy new editions of titles already in the collection, to buy the source in CD-ROM or DVD format, or whether to contract with vendors for online access. Maintaining this diverse reference collection is an ongoing process. Regular inventory of the reference collection is required to identify areas that need to be updated or strengthened.

There are a variety of possible arrangements of reference materials. The arrangement will depend on the library media center, the students served, alignment with the curriculum, as well as personal preferences of the school library media specialist. Blanche Woolls remarks that, "It is time to consider ways to make the entire school the media center" (75). Schools that have adopted a whole language curriculum and teach curriculum across the school *need* to have reference materials away from the central library collection. However, with this philosophy, the school library media specialist must formulate and implement a plan for keeping track of materials such that they can be located quickly and easily. If this option is not currently feasible, one possibility for grouping materials is to maintain a classified arrangement regardless of type. Another alternative is to assemble types of resources together, such as encyclopedias, directories, ready-reference, and the like. However, it is difficult to integrate sources requiring special equipment, such as computer workstations. Of primary importance is ease of access to reference materials by the school library media specialist and the student population.

Conclusion

In order to create and maintain a school reference collection that meets the informational needs of students, effective selection and evaluation of resources by the school library media specialist is essential. Several considerations are important with regard to the selection of reference materials: 1) knowing about the school, the school community, and the student population (input from teachers, staff, and students are also vital). These individuals have content experience/knowledge that a school library media specialist may not have; 2) eliciting the expert advice of the school's faculty members and drawing on their experience and knowledge; and 3) keeping a record of questions asked or research requests. Remember as well that the selection process is a highly individualized one. No two school library media specialists are alike; student needs differ from school to school. Attention should be given not only to known requests, but also to anticipated demands.

Because of the high cost of many reference materials, it is critical that effective evaluation of reference resources occurs by the school library media specialist. Although much judgment is subjective, tools or aids and specific criteria are available to assist with appropriate evaluation of reference sources. In the technologically oriented world of today, evaluation is even more complex and diverse—and much more vital. A thorough knowledge of existing resources, as well as the community and school population served, is crucial to successful evaluation of reference materials. Additionally, experience and practice is significant in making correct decisions. As explained by William A. Katz, "In time the beginner becomes a veteran. And veteran [school library media specialists] never quit; or are fired, or die. They simply gain fame as being among the wisest people in the world. One could do worse" (3).

PART 2

Nuts
and
Bolts

Chapter 3
Bibliographies

Introduction

A bibliography brings order out of chaos. Simply stated, a bibliography is a list of materials. More thorough definitions of the term bibliography are: 1) the history, identification, or description of writings or publications; and 2) a list of descriptive or critical works of writing related to a particular subject, period, or author; a list written by an author or printed by a publishing house. Bibliographies are useful tools; they can tell a user the author of a work, who published the material and when, how much it costs, and so on. The basic purpose remains the same, whether the format is print or electronic.

Bibliographic control refers to two kinds of access to information: bibliographic access (Does the work exist?) and physical access (Where can the work be found?). Providing bibliographic and physical access is achieved through bibliographies, library catalogs, and bibliographic utilities. Bibliographies list materials (or parts of materials) regardless of location; library catalogs list works located in a given library (or libraries); bibliographic utilities serve both functions. Bibliographic utilities are information vendors who provide a centralized database for libraries to catalog, share, and retrieve bibliographic records according to national or international bibliographic standards. Bibliographies and library catalogs can be current or retrospective. Current bibliographies and library catalogs list works close to the time at which they are published. Retrospective bibliographic sources cover materials published during an earlier time.

A universal bibliography (although it is currently a nonexistent entity) would include everything published from the beginning through the present. Time, territory, subject, language, or form would not limit it. Access to the world's information is definitely nearer. It is doubtful that a complete bibliography will be seen in the immediate future; however, almost complete is a reality. This phenomenon is accomplished by having online access to national bibliographies; an example being the Online Computer Library Center (OCLC) found online at www.oclc.org (OCLC First Search at (www.oclc.org/oclc/menu/fs.htm).

Bibliographies can be divided into several different types: national bibliographies, trade bibliographies, library catalogs, union catalogs, and subject catalogs. National bibliographies list materials published in a particular country and are often the product of the government. Current national bibliographies usually appear weekly or monthly with annual or multiyear cumulations. The United States national bibliography is called the National Union Catalog (NUC). It lists all works that are cataloged by the Library of Congress and other members of the system.

Trade bibliographies are commercial publications that include the necessary information to select and purchase recently published materials. Works such as textbooks, government documents, encyclopedias, and dissertations are not included in trade bibliographies. A well-known bibliography of this type is *Books in Print* (BIP). BIP is limited to books available for purchase and contains only printed books (hardbound and paperback).

Library catalogs list materials in the collection of a particular library (such as a school library media center). Because of advanced technologies, many libraries can now provide this information to both local and remote users. These catalogs may also list the collections of other libraries—school library media centers, public libraries, academic libraries, and so on.

Union catalogs identify the materials held in more than one library. Online, through bibliographic utilities (such as OCLC, RLIN, Internet, etc.), it is possible to view holdings in thousands of libraries around the world. The geographic area covered may vary from local to multinational. A useful example for school library media situations is SUNLINK (www.sunlink.ucf.edu), a Florida project that enables students to use curriculum and information resources, skills, and strategies to become successful. Universal access stations have been established in 24 Florida schools.

Subject bibliographies are lists of materials that relate to a specific topic; they are intended for those researching special areas. Hundreds of subject bibliographies exist; many follow the same pattern of organization and presentation. Various disciplines and large areas of knowledge have their own bibliographies (see "Examples of Subject Bibliographies.")

Examples of Subject Bibliographies

Native Americans—Internet Resources
   http://falcon.jmu.edu/~ramseyil/native.htm
   *This site is offered by the Internet School Library Media Center,
   providing bibliographies, directories to pages of tribes, history and
   historical documents, periodicals, and general links.*

Bibliographies of the War of American Independence
   http://www.army.mil/cmh-pg/reference/revbib/revwar.htm
   *This Web site provides bibliographies that were originally produced by
   the US Army Center of Military History, Historical Resources Branch.*

Classic Bibliographies Online
   www.williams.edu/Classics/biblio.html
   *This site includes Literature Bibliographies, the Ancient Mediterranean,
   Greek and Roman History, and Greek and Latin Language.*

Dream Gate and Electric Dreams
   http://dreamgate.com/dream/bibs/
   *This Web site offers a collection of bibliographies of dream researchers,
   clinicians, dream workers, anthropologists, and other dream-concerned
   individuals and groups.*

Online Chaucer Bibliographies
   www.unc.edu/depts/chaucer/chbib.htm
   *This site provides an organized navigation aid for Chaucer resources on
   the Web, including Chaucer Pages, Chaucer Works, Life and Times, and
   so forth.*

Evaluation and Selection

Evaluation of Bibliographies

AUTHORITY:
- The compilers or authors should possess the academic backgrounds or academic structure to justify their roles in writing a bibliography
- Look for reputable publishers of bibliographies, such as Brodart and H. W. Wilson
- It is important to verify the reputation of lesser-known publishers

FREQUENCY:
- The source should be current when that is the purpose of the bibliography

ORGANIZATION:
- The source should be organized in a clear, user-friendly fashion, with indexes that complement the arrangement
- Explicit explanations regarding how to use the work should be included

SCOPE:
- The scope should be stated in the introduction or preface
- Consult guides to the reference works that give concise, unambiguous descriptions of coverage, accuracy, and intent

---

When evaluating bibliographies, the following criteria should be used: authority, frequency, organization, and scope. Authority relates to the qualifications of the compiler or the author. The compilers or authors should possess the educational backgrounds and/or academic structure to justify their roles in writing a bibliography. As with all reference areas, reputable publishers of bibliographies exist, such as R. R. Bowker, Brodart, and H. W. Wilson. It is advisable to verify the reputation of lesser-known publishers through review tools and aids. A bibliography should be current when this is the purpose of the bibliography. Currentness also refers to the delay between the date of publication of the material to be listed and the time at which it entered in the bibliography. Frequency is most applicable when selecting current bibliographies. It is important to note that often the same work has a different updating schedule in each of its formats. Bibliographies will vary widely in organization or arrangement. However, all bibliographies should be organized in a clear, user-friendly fashion with indexes that complement the arrangement. In addition, the compiler should offer explicit explanations regarding how to effectively use the work. Bibliographies must be as complete as possible within their stated purposes. In the introduction or preface, the compiler should state the scope of the bibliography. It is also valuable to consult guides to the reference works that give concise and unambiguous descriptions of coverage, accuracy, and intent.

The selection of bibliographies for a school library media center situation depends on the needs—both known and anticipated—of the school, community, and student population served. Before selecting a specific bibliography, it is advisable to read the introduction and several entries. It may also be helpful to ask the following questions: Does the bibliography meet identified needs? Are the directions accurate and the explanations clear? Is the bibliography available in several formats? Is the coverage inclusive for the intended purposes? Is it evident why the items are included in the bibliography? Is the bibliography well organized and user friendly? Remain aware of the overall purpose of bibliographies—to provide information about the availability of materials, their costs, and whether they are recommended (although not all bibliographic tools include this element).

Basic Sources

There are several well-known, basic bibliographies for libraries. It is valuable and helpful to become familiar with these reference tools, although your school library media center situation may not require, nor have the budget to purchase such resources.

The *American Book Publishing Record* (ABPR), published by R. R. Bowker, is a monthly publication that includes complete cataloging records for books as they are published.

The *American Reference Books Annual* (ARBA), an annual publication by Libraries Unlimited, Inc., analyzes more than 1,500 reference titles. This tool is limited to titles published or distributed in the United States and Canada. ARBA is comprehensive and includes annotations written by subject experts.

Books in Print (BIP), published annually by R. R. Bowker, is a listing of books available from United States publishers. This bibliography is available online (www.booksinprint.com) and in print and DISC formats. BIP includes more than one million citations; thousands of new titles are added annually. BIP is updated with the *Books in Print Supplement,* which appears approximately six months after the main volumes of BIP. *Children's Books in Print* includes more than 100,000 in-print titles as well as videos and audiocassettes. This bibliography, published annually, is available online, as well as in print and DISC formats. *Paperbound Books in Print* supplies information regarding United States paperback titles. *Forthcoming Books in Print* is a bimonthly supplement that lists new books in print, as well as those projected for publication within the upcoming several months. Four additional BIP titles include *Global Books in Print,* a host of English-language books, audios, and videos offered online at www.globalbooksinprint.com (also on DISC); *Spanish Books in Print,* which includes more than 1.5 million Spanish entries (online and DISC formats); *Patron Books in Print*, their newest version designed to meet the needs of library patrons (online format); and *Books Out of Print*, which reaches as far back as the 1920s (online format).

Book Review Digest Plus, a quarterly publication (recently expanded), is available online via (www.hwwilson.com), in print (published by H. W. Wilson), and CD-ROM formats. This bibliographic database contains more than 50,000 English language fiction and nonfiction titles.

Guide to Reference Books, an American Library Association publication lists and annotates more than 15,000 titles that are arranged under main sections; it provides an inclusive index.

Literary Market Place, published annually by R. R. Bowker, provides current data on publishers, including more than 15,000 listings. It is available in print and CD-ROM formats, as well as online (www.literarymarketplace.com).

The *National Union Catalog* (NUC) began as the actual card catalog of the Library of Congress. Later, due to the need for increased access, duplicates of the cards were created, distributed, and maintained by large United States research libraries. The NUC can be accessed online via OCLC First Search; fee-based updates vary according to the period covered.

The *Union List of Serials in Libraries of the United States and Canada* (ULS) is published by H. W. Wilson and contains, in alphabetical order by main entry serials published before 1950. As the title indicates, it is limited to serials published in the United States and Canada.

Of particular importance to school library media centers, the following *examples* of bibliographies may also be thought of as selection tools. There are numerous works of this nature; these are merely a sampling of bibliographies that are valuable for school library media centers. It is important to purchase these resources carefully, as they are essential for effective collection development.

The *Middle and Junior High School Library Catalog* and *the Senior High School Library Catalog* are bibliographies of recommended titles appropriate for middle and high school students; H. W. Wilson publishes them both. Additional examples of bibliographies suitable for school library media center situations are*: A to Zoo: Subject Access to Children's Picture Books* (R. R. Bowker*), Best Books for Children* (R. R. Bowker), *Best Books for Young Adult Readers* (R. R. Bowker*), and *A Guide to Reference Materials for School Library Media Centers* (Libraries Unlimited, Inc.).

Due to the emergence of new and exciting technologies, numerous bibliographies are available online at no cost. For example, many states currently have virtual libraries. These online libraries provide valuable information and are significant resources that should not be overlooked for school library media centers. Other examples of valuable online sources are: 1) *Bookwire* (www.bookwire.com) by R. R. Bowker, claims to be the most comprehensive online information source. It includes timely book industry news, features, reviews, guides to literary events, author interviews, and thousands of annotated links to book-related sites (*Bookwire* now includes PubEasy and Pubnet); and 2) *The Internet Library for Librarians* (www.itcompany.com/inforetriever). This online source provides information about library vendors, publishers, booksellers, and distributors, as well as an abundance of information regarding specific school library media and reference resources.

A wealth of information is at our fingertips; at times it may seem too much. Bibliographies, however, can organize this data into meaningful, valuable units—and eliminate chaos and provide order.

Webliography

Books in Print
> www.booksinprint.com
> *This is the largest Web-based bibliographic resource for professionals, including an authoritative and comprehensive database of more than five million books, audio books, and video titles.*

Book Review Digest Plus
> www.hwwilson.com
> *Via this Web site, one can retrieve book summaries, bibliographic data, full-text reviews, review excerpts, or basic citations encompassing more than 1,200,000 reviews coving more than a half million books.*

BookWire
> www.bookwire.com
> *More than 8,000 links; ranked in the top 100,000 most visited Web sites listed in Alexa; a comprehensive online portal into the book industry, providing librarians, publishers, booksellers, authors, and general book enthusiasts with resources they need.*

Global Books in Print
> www.globalbooksinprint.com
> *This site offers English-language books, audios, and videos in: BIP Alert Service, Forthcoming Book Room, Children's Room, Fiction Room and more.*

Internet Library for Librarians
> www.itcompany.com/inforetriever
> *This Web site is a portal designed for librarians to locate Internet resources related to their profession.*

Literary Market Place
> www.literarymarketplace.com
> *This is a fee-based site; a worldwide resource for the book publishing industry.*

OCLC First Search
> www.oclc.org/oclc/menu/fs.htm
> *This online service gives users access to a collection of reference databases; FirstSearch materials in your library's collection are highlighted in results from searches in dozens of leading databases.*

Online Computer Library Center (OCLC)
> www.oclc.org
> *This Web site is a Worldwide Library Cooperative, offering: OCLC Worldwide, Librarian's Toolbox, Resources, and more.*

SUNLINK

www.sunlink.ucf.edu

This site includes more than one million titles from approximately 2,000 K-12 schools in the state of Florida, more than 16,000 Web sites and nearly 300,000 book jacket cover images.

Chapter *4*

Directories, Almanacs, Yearbooks, and Handbooks

Introduction

One person's trivia is another person's main interest. Directories, almanacs, handbooks, and yearbooks primarily answer ready-reference questions. Ready-reference is all about facts. A fact book is a publication containing information organized in a systematic way. As stated in Dickens' *Hard Times*, "Now what I want is facts…facts alone are wanted in life." A ready-reference question may only take a minute or two to answer; however, it may develop into a complex search. For example, a student who requests the address of a specific college may actually not only want the address, but also information about how to apply to the college and other related data. The purpose of this chapter is to provide an overview of these four reference tools, their chief uses, selection procedures, considerations for evaluation, and examples of sources used in school library media centers.

      Directories are defined by the *ALA Glossary of Library and Information Science* as, "A list of persons or organizations, systematically arranged, usually in alphabetic or classed order, giving address, affiliations, etc. for individuals, and address, officers, functions, and similar data for organizations" (Strayer 75). This definition is a pure one; it should be noted that aside from directories themselves, numerous other ready-reference tools have sections devoted to directory information. Directories are used to locate and verify names of phenomena, as well as to match individuals with organizations. Students often wish to locate other people, experts, organizations, and institutions through addresses, phone numbers, zip codes, titles, names, and so on. Directories are the most rapid and effective method of obtaining this sort of information. Less obvious uses of directories include limited biographical information about an individual and information about an institution or political group. Because directories are closely concerned with humans and their organizations, they can serve numerous uses. Although directories can be divided into a number of categories, the following are six basic types: government, institutional, investment, local, professional, and trade and business.

Almanacs, yearbooks, and handbooks provide factual information about numerous items, such as people, organizations, things, current and historical events, countries, governments, and statistical trends. Many other sources also offer this type of information; however, almanacs, yearbooks, and handbooks are more convenient sources of this data. Often these sources are single volumes that summarize and synthesize large amounts of information.

An almanac is a resource that provides useful data and statistics related to countries, personalities, events, and subjects. It is a publication containing astronomical and meteorological data arranged according to days, weeks, and months of a given year, and often including a miscellany of other information. Almost every school library media center can benefit from having a general almanac. A paperbound edition of many almanacs costs less than twenty dollars. The most famous early almanac was Benjamin Franklin's *Poor Richard's Almanac*, published from 1732 to 1748. *Old Farmer's Almanac* is an example of this type of almanac that currently continues to be published. Although almanacs can be extensive in geographical coverage, many of the best-known general almanacs are inclined towards a specific country or state. An almanac can answer questions such as the following: Where was George W. Bush born? What is the population of Oman? Which NCAA Division 1 team has won the most regular season games? How much saturated fat is in a pound of butter? What is the address of the American Embassy in Italy?

Yearbooks present facts and statistics for a single year (primarily the year preceding the publication date). Encyclopedias often issue yearbooks that supplement the main set and are fundamentally the review of a specific year. A yearbook's primary purpose is to record the year's activities by country, subject, or specialized area. A general yearbook is the place to find information on topics such as the winner of an athletic event of that year, an obituary for a notable person who died during the year, or the description of a catastrophe that occurred that particular year.

Handbooks are sometimes called manuals; they serve as guides to a particular subject. Often large amounts of information about a subject are compressed into a single volume. The content and organization of handbooks may vary widely. The basic purpose of handbooks is as ready-reference sources for given fields of knowledge. With a few exceptions, most handbooks have a limited scope. Their particular value is depth of information in a narrow field. There are countless handbooks available; school library media specialists should select specific ones based on ease of arrangement and amount of use. Handbooks provide answers to questions such as these: How do I cite references within the text in MLA format? Who wrote the poem, The Raven? Is single or double-spacing used when writing a research paper? Who is known as the Greek Goddess of Love?

Facts that answer ready-reference questions are a major part of reference services in school library media centers. Providing ample, as well as suitable, resources of this type are essential for any school collection. Although certain factual information can be located in other reference sources, it is always beneficial to have basic directories, almanacs, yearbooks, and handbooks (in all formats) available to meet the informational needs of students.

Evaluation and Selection

Evaluation of Directories, Almanacs, Yearbooks, and Handbooks

SCOPE:
- The source should determine what is covered—organizations, geographic areas, individuals, etc.
- The comprehensiveness of the source should be evident within the stated scope.
- The title, preface, or introductory materials often gives pertinent information.

CURRENCY:
- Note the frequency of the publication and how often it is updated.

ACCURACY:
- This is the most important characteristic of works that present factual information.
- Test accuracy by reading reviews, comparing data from different sources, and relying on experts in the field.
- The statistics should be recent and from official, identified sources.

FORMAT:
- Entries should be clearly arranged and organized in a logical manner, consistent throughout the source.
- The index in a fact source should be helpful, accurate, and consistent in style and terminology.

The general rules of evaluating any reference work are applicable to directories, almanacs, yearbooks, and handbooks as well. To some degree, we all rely on what reference materials state as facts; however, these should be tested regularly. Is it a fact or an opinion? Is the fact no longer a fact? For instance, at one time in our history, it was a fact that the world was flat. Due to discoveries and experiments, this fact is no longer true—no longer a fact. An effective method of checking a fact is to find its original source. The reference source should clearly indicate where the information was obtained. The following criteria are useful in evaluating directories, almanacs, yearbooks, and handbooks:

> **Scope**: What exactly is covered? What organizations, geographic areas, or types of individuals are included in the resource? How comprehensive is the source within its stated scope? The title many times gives insight into

the scope of a source; the preface (or introductory materials in electronic sources) will often provide even more detailed information.

Currency: What is the frequency of the publication? How often is it updated? Almanacs, yearbooks, and titles that are updated once a year typically overcome this dilemma; this is also true of online resources.

Accuracy: Accuracy is the single most important characteristic of works that present factual information. How is the information in the source updated? Numerous methods are used in updating records, such as verifying by telephone, examining public records, and so on. To test accuracy, one can read reviews, compare data from different sources, and rely on experts in the field. Many of these reference resources are composed, in part, of second-hand information. The statistics should be recent and from official sources; those sources should be identified. Reference works without documentation are of questionable validity.

Format: Are the entries clearly arranged, organized in a logical manner, and consistent throughout the source? Indexes are a significant factor in providing access to the information it includes. The index in a fact source should be helpful, accurate, and consistent in style and terminology. A major consideration is the availability of the resource in electronic format (CD-ROM, DVD, online, etc.). Electronic formats may contain more current information than their printed counterparts. Electronic versions can cumulate a number of years and eliminate the need to consult numerous volumes. Electronic sources can often be searched more efficiently. Keyword searching is helpful. By keyword searching, the exact names or titles need not be known. Additionally, electronic searching provides the ability to combine fields or terms (using Boolean logic, quotation marks, and so on). The obvious disadvantage of using electronic sources is the cost involved (hardware, software, connectivity time). This should be weighed against the advantages of speed and the currency of the information accessed.

School library media specialists should select all reference sources—including directories, almanacs, yearbooks, and handbooks—such that they answer the information requests of students. These types of resources will vary greatly from library to library. Sources included in a school library media center collection should be based on the students and community served, the types of questions asked, and the number of questions posed in a particular subject area (curriculum needs). Another critical factor in the selection process is the geographic location of the school. This may dictate a concentration of sources dealing with a specific locality. The budget available must obviously be taken into account. Decisions about which of the specialized directories, almanacs, yearbooks, and handbooks to purchase are not as easily made as the decision to buy general sources of these types. These four reference tools offer a very good value at a low cost. However, school library media centers generally have smaller collections of this nature than public and larger academic libraries. The age and level of the student population affects the resources selected. As with all reference resources, review journals—tools and aids—are available to assist with the proper and efficient evaluation and selection of directories, almanacs, yearbooks, and handbooks.

Basic Sources

The directories, almanacs, yearbooks, and handbooks discussed in this chapter include a sampling of the sources appropriate for school library media centers. Actual selections will depend on your distinctive school situation. It should also be noted that these types of resources are not as plentiful (or used) in elementary levels as they are in secondary library media centers.

DIRECTORIES

Two obvious and well-used local directories are the telephone book and the city directory. Although offered separately in print format, they are now combined on CD-ROM and online (www.555-1212.com). *The National Directory of Addresses and Telephone Numbers* published biannually by Omnigraphics, is another directory of this type. It contains more than 100,000 telephone numbers of businesses and government agencies across the United States. Additionally, fax numbers, addresses, zip codes, and toll-free numbers are provided. This directory is available in print and CD-ROM formats. *The AT&T 800 Toll-Free Directory*, published irregularly by AT&T (1992 to present), includes AT&T residential and business toll-free numbers; it is free of charge. This directory is also available online at (http://www.business.att.com/products/productdetails.jsp?productId=tfs). Also sponsored by AT&T, the *AnyWho Directory* is yet another useful directory for the location of telephone numbers and related data. By using the online *AnyWho Directory* (www.anywho.com), one can locate e-mail addresses, homepages, and toll-free numbers. This directory includes more than 90 million entries. *Americom Area Decoder* (http://decoder.americom.com/) is another online telephone directory. By entering a major city name, one can locate the area code, or by entering the area code, the major cities within that area can be found.

Literary Market Place, published annually by R. R. Bowker, is the ultimate directory (guide) to the United States book publishing industry. It includes more than 400,000 publishers and 12,000 firms that are directly or indirectly involved with book publishing in the United States, covering a multiplicity of aspects regarding the publishing business. *Literary Market Place* is available in print format (two volumes), on CD-ROM, and online (www.literarymarketplace.com). *BookWire* (www.bookwire.com), an online source regarding book-related sites (mentioned in chapter 3), is also a valuable resource for information regarding book publishing and related topics.

Numerous college and university directories exist that are extremely valuable for secondary school library media centers. Some of the more well-known ones include *Peterson's College Database*, published annually by Peterson's in CD-ROM format (1987 to present); Peterson's online version (www.petersons.com/ugrad), *Lovejoy's College Guide*, published semiannually by Monarch Press (1949 to present, print format); *Lovejoy's College Counselor*, the CD-ROM equivalent published annually by Intermedia Active Software, and *The College Handbook*, published by the College Board (various dates) available in print format and on CD-ROM. Numerous online directories are valuable resources when searching for college and university information. *College Net* (www.collegenet.com) claims to be the number one portal for applying to colleges over the Web. It includes more than 300 colleges and universities. *All About College* (www.allaboutcollege.com) offers thousands of links to colleges and universities around the world, as well as admissions office e-mail addresses for most schools. *The Admissions Office* (www.theadmissionsoffice.com) links to hundreds of colleges and universities. This Web site also offers the Live Internet Selection Assistance (LISA), a college counselor who provides short answers to general questions by users. Secondary students often request information about specific colleges and universities; these directories are very beneficial in answering questions of this nature.

An example of a statistical directory often used in library media centers is the *Statistical Abstract of the United States*. This directory, a basic source of American statistical data, contains a collection of statistics on social and economic conditions in the United States as well as selected international data. *Statistical Abstract of the United States* is published annually and is available online (http://www.census.gov/statab/www/) and in both print (published by the Government Printing Office) and CD-ROM (published by the Bureau of the Census) formats.

The Encyclopedia of Associations is a directory published five times a year by Gale Research, Inc., which lists and describes more than 20,000 associations and organizations. Broad subjects with detailed indexes divide this directory; a typical entry covers 15 to 20 basic points about the association or organization. This is available in print format (three volumes) and on CD-ROM (the equivalent of 13 print volumes).

Directories are typically user-friendly reference tools. The scope is normally indicated in the title and the kind of information is limited and typically presented in an orderly, clear manner.

ALMANACS

Where a single figure or fact is required, the almanac can be very useful. Students enjoy facts and trivia; therefore, almanacs are wonderful sources for browsing, as well as information seeking. *The World Almanac and Book of Facts*, published annually by Funk and Wagnall's (1868 to present, print format and via various online databases), provides brief, accurate essay pieces on topics of current interest. This almanac includes a quick reference index with approximately 80 broad subject headings; it also provides a section on maps and flags. Microsoft Corporation publishes annually its CD-ROM equivalent, *The World Almanac*. *Information Please Almanac*, published annually by Houghton Mifflin Company, is yet another popular almanac for school library media centers. *Information Please* (1974 to present) features discursive, larger units on such subjects as the lively arts, science, education, and medicine. The make up of this almanac is considerably more attractive, with larger type and spacing than *The World Almanac*. The *Information Please Almanac* is also available online (www.infoplease.com) as is the *Information Please Kids Almanac* (www.kids.infoplease.com). *The Daily Almanac* provides interesting facts about today's date. It includes categories such as Today's Figures, Today's Fun Facts, Today's Horoscope, Births, Deaths, and Special Events. *The Daily Almanac* is available online (http://www.infoplease.com/cgi-bin/daily?link=tmplnav).

Multitudes of specialized almanacs are available; many of them suitable for school library media centers. The following are examples of almanacs of a specific nature. The *Almanac of American Politics* (National Journal) provides colorful profiles and insightful analysis of all members of Congress as well as governors. This almanac is arranged by state, name, and house committees. It is easily searchable and updated frequently. The *Writer's Almanac*, available online at (www.writersalmanac.org), can also be heard each day on public radio stations throughout the United States. This almanac is a daily program of poetry and history provided by Garrison Keillor. The *World Almanac of Presidential Quotations* (Pharos Book/St. Martin's Press), *The People's Almanac Presents Presidents of the Twentieth Century* (Little, Brown, & Company), and *The World Almanac and Book of Facts 2000* (World Almanac) are examples of the numerous useful almanacs for secondary school library media centers. *Information Please Environmental Almanac* (World Resources Institute) and *Almanac of the 50 States* (Information Publishing, 2000) are examples of almanacs particularly suitable for elementary school library media centers. Almanacs valuable for your specific school situation should be determined using appropriate selection and evaluation tools and aids, aligning them with the specific curriculum and information needs of your school population.

YEARBOOKS

Almost every imaginable area of human interest has its own yearbook. There are literally hundreds of yearbooks available. The following are four examples of yearbooks appropriate for school library media centers. *Facts on File* is a weekly digest of information covering political, social, cultural, and athletic events. *Facts on File*, published by Facts on File (print format), contains weekly issues that are placed in a yearly loose-leaf volume. This yearbook is also available on CD-ROM, which cumulates the full text of News Digest from 1980 to present. *Facts on File* is also available online (www.facts.com). *Facts on File News Services* (or Facts.com) is an excellent fee-based online source (www.2facts.com). This resource brings together content from seven core reference databases to answer questions about events, issues, statistics, and people of the last 20 years. It includes 200 biographies, more than 100 key events, overviews of 50 controversial issues, and thousands of hyperlinks. *Facts.com* is appropriate for middle and high school students; it introduces young adults to people and events that have shaped and are shaping our world. The cost is reasonable for school libraries and the scope of content is very broad. *The Statesman's Yearbook*, published annually by St. Martin's Press, Inc., provides concise but complete descriptions of organizations and countries. It emphasizes the political and economic aspects of the world from 1864 to present. *The American Book of Days*, published by H. W. Wilson and updated infrequently, discusses how and why holidays are celebrated. Beneath each day of the year this yearbook lists major and minor events, many of which are explained in detailed essays.

Common types of yearbooks, not to be overlooked for school library media centers, are encyclopedia yearbooks, published with most major encyclopedias. Encyclopedia yearbooks are resources that identify names, dates, statistics, events, and other important items of the preceding year. These yearbooks, however, are being published less often with the integration of electronic sources.

HANDBOOKS

Handbooks provide information about given fields of knowledge; they zero in on a specific area of interest. There are numerous handbooks and manuals, ranging from nature study to classical mythology. The handbooks purchased should be of value and interest to your school, community, and student population. *The Guinness Book of Records*, published annually by Facts on File, is probably the most famous handbook. It was first published in 1956 and is divided into chapters pertaining to specific subjects, such as living world and human beings. This handbook is now available on CD-ROM and is entitled, *The Guinness Disc of Records* that is published annually by Grolier Electronic Publishing; it is now offered online, as well. There are many specific Guinness titles now published on a variety of topics, such as rock stars, names, and speed. *Famous First Facts, 4th edition*, published by H. W. Wilson, is another popular handbook for school library media centers. *Famous First Facts* is just that—an alphabetical subject list of first happenings, discoveries, and inventions in American history.

Masterplots II, published by Salem Press in its Definitive Revised Edition (CD-ROM format) is a popular handbook with secondary school students. It provides plot summaries for more than 2,000 books, and is a condensation of almost every important classic in the English Language. *Monarch Notes* (CD-ROM format published by the Bureau of Electronic Publishing), similar to *Masterplots II*, is useful for a summary of plot or content, character analyses, commentary on the text, and author background data. Online sources include, for example, *Spark Notes* (www.sparknotes.com), which is extremely useful for students.

Occupational Outlook Handbook, published biennially by the Government Printing Office, is also a well-used resource among secondary students. This handbook, published by the United States Department of Labor, provides detailed descriptions of more than 300 occupations, covering 85 percent of all jobs in the United States. Each essay within *Occupational Outlook Handbook* indicates what a job is likely to offer in advancement, employment, location, earnings, and working conditions. The CD-ROM equivalent is entitled *Occupational Outlook DISCovering Careers and Jobs* and is published annually by Gale Research, Inc. *Occupational Outlook Handbook* is also available online (http://www.bls.gov/oco/home.htm). A youth version is available at (http://www.dol.gov/dol/audience/aud-kidsyouth.htm).

Bartlett's Familiar Quotations, published by Little, Brown, and Co. (print format), is by far the most famous book of quotations. This handbook, including more than 2,000 individuals and 20,000 quotations, is a collection of passages, phrases, and proverbs traced to their sources in ancient and modern times. *Bartlett's* (the older version) can also be found online at (www.bartleby.com/99/index.html).

Published by the Oxford University Press, *The Oxford Dictionary of Quotations* is also a popular book of quotations found in many school library media centers. It includes more than 15,000 quotations; it is international in scope. An example of a current online quotation resource is Michael Moncur's *The Quotations Page* (www.starlingtech.com/quotes), a catalog of quotation resources on the Internet.

As previously mentioned, there are numerous handbooks covering an enormous range of topics. The following are examples of handbooks, illustrating the wide variety available for school library media centers today: *MLA Handbook for Writers of Research Papers* (Modern Language Association of America); *Publication*

Manual of the American Psychological Association (American Psychological Association); *Mayo Clinic Family Health Book* (print, William Morrow; CD-ROM, IVI Publishing); *Physicians' Desk Reference* (print is published annually by Medical Economics Data and CD-ROM published quarterly); *The New Century Handbook of English Literature* (Appleton-Century Crof); *The American Inventors Instructional Handbook* (Dealco Manufacturing); *21st Century Grammar Handbook* (Dell Publishing Co.); *AIDS Crisis in America: A Reference Handbook* (ABC-CLIO); *2000 Handbook of United States Coins* (Golden Books Publishing Company); and *101 Creative Problem-Solving Techniques: The Handbook of New Ideas for Business* (New Management Publishing Company).

There are countless directories, almanacs, yearbooks, and handbooks. New ones, as well as old ones in new formats, appear each year. It is obviously impossible to list all of them. In practice, as a school library media specialist, these reference sources should be selected primarily because they meet student's informational needs—but also because they portray the uniqueness of the school, student population, and community served.

More Examples of Online Directories, Almanacs, Yearbooks, and Handbooks

Big Yellow
> www.bigyellow.com
> *This Web site provides maps, driving directions, global directories, and much more.*

The College Press Network
> www.cpnet.com
> *Via this site, one can search Travel, Finance, Insurance, Health, Internet, Education, Business, Legal, Cars, and so forth.*

Consumer Reports
> www.consumerreports.com
> *ConsumerReport.org is fee-based. From this site, one can search automobiles, appliances, computers, health and fitness, personal finance, etc.*

Embarrassing Problems
> www.embarrassingproblems.co.uk
> *This Web site proclaims, "Straight-talking, good-advise." It offers, for example, A Problem Solved, Previous Problems, a list of areas from which to choose.*

Fed Stats
> www.fedstats.gov
> *This site provides Links to Statistics and Links to Statistical Agencies—from over 100 U.S. Federal agencies.*

Find Law

www.findlaw.com
This Web site provides Legal News, For Legal Professionals, For Students, For the Public, For Businesses, and many other useful links.

Food and Drug Administration
www.fda.gov/default.htm
This site includes Products FDA Regulates, A-Z Index, Food Industry, Hot Topics, FDA Activities, and more.

Guinness World Records
www.guinessworldrecords.com
This online version offers a free newsletter; one can search areas such as Human Body, Amazing Feats, Natural World, Science and Technology, Arts and Media, and so on.

The Monster Board
www.monster.com
Via this Web site, one can apply for Online Jobs, Have Jobs E-mailed to You, Let A Company Find You, Search anywhere in the U.S. for a job, get career advice, etc.

Mayo Health Oasis
www.mayohealth.org
This site includes areas such as Diseases and Conditions, Drug Search, Health Tools, Healthy Living, Books and Newsletters (one newsletter is free).

The Old Farmer's Almanac
www.almanac.com
This Web site offers information about Astronomy, Weather, Gardening, Food, Press, Shop, Today in History, and more.

PDR Net
www.pdr.net
This site is fee-based. It includes Drug Information, Medical References, Patient Education, Medical Marketplace, and much more.

People Finder
www.peoplefinder.com
This Web site offers People Search, People Finder, Background checks, court Records; it also locates "best finders and prices."

PubMed
www.ncbi.nlm.nih.gov/entrez/query.fcgi?db=PubMed
This online site is fee-based and is offered by the National Library of Medicine. It includes more than 14 million citations for biomedical articles from MEDLINE and other life science journals.

Reference: Best Sources for Facts on the Net

www.refdesk.com
This Web site offers Search RefDesk, Search Dictionary, Search Thesaurus, In the News, Local News, Today in History, Current Events Topics, and more.

Snopes
www.snopes.com
This interesting site includes, for example, Urban Legends Reference page, Autos, Music, Luck, Business, Horrors, Humor, Holidays, and Military.

Standard & Poor's Register
www.standardpoor.com
This famous Web site is a provider of credit ratings and other financial products and services.

Who Where?
www.whowhere.lycos.com
This site searches more than 100,000 databases and resources, including public records.

Webliography

The Admissions Office
www.theadmissionsoffice.com
This Web site links to hundreds of colleges and universities, with "live Internet selection assistance."

Americom Area Decoder
http://decoder.americom.com
This online telephone directory assists one in locating area codes, cities, and so forth.

All About College
www.allaboutcollege.com
This site offers thousands of links to colleges and universities, as well as an admissions office, email addresses, and much more.

AnyWho Directory
www.anywho.com
Via this online site, one can locate email addresses, homepages, and toll-free numbers.

AT&T 800 Toll-Free Directory
www.business.att.com/products/productdetails.jsp?productId=tfs
This Web site includes AT&T residential and business toll-free numbers—free of charge.

Bartlett's Familiar Quotations

www.bartleby.com/99/index.html
This online site offers more than 2,000 individuals and 20,000 quotations, phrases, and proverbs.

BookWire
www.bookwire.com
This Web site is an extremely valuable online source regarding book-related sites.

College Net
www.collegenet.com
This Web site claims to be the number one portal for applying to colleges over the Web—a very useful online source.

Daily Almanac
www.infoplease.com/cgi-bin/daily?link=tmplnav
This site provides interesting facts about today's date, such as Today's Figures, Today's Fun Facts, Today's Horoscope, Special Events and so on.

Facts on File
www.facts.com
This online source offers accumulations of full-text articles from "News Digest."

Facts on File News Services
www.2facts.com
This fee-based source answers questions about events, issues, statistics, etc. from the last 20 years.

Information Please Almanac
www.infoplease.com
This Web site features such subjects as arts, science, education, and medicine.

Information Please Kids Almanac
www.kids.infoplease.com
This online source is a kid-friendly version of Information Please.

Literary Market Place
www.literarymarketplace.com
This notable Web site is a guide to the United States book publishing industry.

Occupational Outlook Handbook
www.bls.gov/oco/home.htm
This site provides detailed descriptions of more than 300 occupations.

Peterson's College Database

www.petersons.com/ugrad
This online resource offers an inclusive list of colleges and universities.

The Quotations Page
www.starlingtech.com/quotes
The Quotations Page is an online catalog of quotation resources on the Internet.

Statistical Abstract of the United States
www.census.gov/statab/www
This Web site is a basic source of American statistical data—containing a collection of statistics about social and economic conditions in the U.S. and internationally.

Telephone Book and City Directory
www.555-1212.com
This online source is a local directory, offering a telephone book and city directory.

Chapter 5

Biographical Sources

Introduction

People are interesting; learning about individuals is fascinating. Students learn about people because they are curious and want to discover what others are like and have accomplished. What do biographical sources do? What is their purpose? Biographies tell about what people have done or what they are doing, whether it is their occupation, date of birth, major accomplishments, or their life in general. They are sources of fact as well as pictures of everyday life. As explained by William A. Katz (2002), "In reference work, the primary use of biography is: 1) to locate people who are famous in a given occupation, career, or profession; 2) to locate supporting material about an individual for any number of reasons from a paper on the fall of Rome to a study on the modern automobile's brake system; and not the least, 3) to locate a possible name for a baby."

Types of Biographical Sources

Two basic types of biographical sources are available: direct and indirect. Direct sources provide factual information about a person, such as date of birth, date of death, place of birth, career history, etc. Well-known examples of direct sources are *Current Biography* and *Who's Who*. Indirect sources list bibliographic citations leading the student to other works that may contain the information sought. Typically these sources are indexes to other sources. *Biography Index* (H. W. Wilson Company), *World Biography Index* (K. G. Saur North America) and *Biography Master Index* (Gale Group) are examples of online indirect sources. These two types of biographical sources can be further divided into two categories: current and retrospective. Current sources provide information about living persons; retrospective sources supply information about historical figures. Some biographical tools give data on both living and dead individuals. Regardless of type or category, biographical sources vary in extent and coverage. Some sources, for example, focus on one profession or academic field, such as *American Presidents: Life Portraits*, which can be found online (www.americanpresidents.org) or *Contemporary Authors* (Gale Group) located online at (http://contemporarylit.about.com/cs/authors/). Another class of biographies includes prominent figures from all fields that live in a specific geographic location, such as *Who's Who in the East* [America] (Marquis Who's Who Reed Reference Publishing). Biographical sources can also be international in scope. The interest in the lives of others is universal; as a result, biographical sources are an essential and significant reference tool for school library media specialists.

Evaluation and Selection

Evaluation of Biographical Sources

COST:
- Determine the most useful format in relation to your budget.
- Consider one-volume sources as opposed to full-volume sets.
- Always take into account the needs of the school and student population.

ACCURACY:
- Note that primary resources may have items omitted.
- Also note that secondary resources may be incorrect or biased.

COMPREHENSIVENESS:
- The criteria for inclusion should be included in the prefatory material.
- The scope and criterion should be in agreement.

EASE-OF-USE:
- The source should be concise, organized, and straightforward.
- Indexes and cross references should be included.

CURRENCY:
- Compare sources with other similar resources to determine if it is up-to-date.
- Check publisher frequency.

How does a school library media specialist know if a biographical source is legitimate, authoritative, and based on accurate material? One hint: The title should be listed in basic bibliographies, such as *Guide to Reference Books* and *American Reference Books Annual*. The publisher's name is another indication of authority. Four popular publishers of biographies are Gale Group, H. W. Wilson Company, St. Martin's Press, and Reed Reference Publishing. As with all other references sources for school library media centers, evaluation and selection of appropriate biographical items must be based on the needs of the school, students, and community. These sources vary widely according to age level, location of school, and numerous other variables. Students require biographies for research purposes, general information needs, as well as to satisfy their personal curiosity. Both current and retrospective biographical sources are essential tools in library media centers.

An overriding factor regarding selection of biographical sources is cost. As a school library media specialist, you must consider the importance of purchasing full-volume sets or a concise one-volume source. You must also decide which format will be most useful in relation to the cost. Should the biographical source be print, a CD-ROM, or purchased as an online resource? These issues must be weighed according to budget and needs of the student population. Does your library media center have the hardware to warrant the purchase of CD-ROMs and online services? Are the students capable of efficiently and effectively searching electronically? Many biographical sources are available in several formats. *American Men and Women of Science* by R. R. Bowker, for instance, is offered in print format (eight volumes), on CD-ROM (entitled *New Scientist*, published quarterly), and online. Some sources remain available in print format only, although this is changing rapidly. Obviously, searching an electronic format is typically more thorough than searching a print source. In addition, one is able to scan thousands of possibilities in seconds, rather than laboriously searching individual indexes and sources. Electronic sources can also include video clips, links to other Web sites, and so forth, which are additional advantages. Your school, students, community, cost, and individuality of your library media center will all play a role in the effective selection of biographical sources.

How does a school library media specialist know if a biographical source, print or electronic, is legitimate and accurate? As with other reference tools, biographical sources should be evaluated as to their accuracy, comprehensiveness, and ease of use. For current resources, the information must be as up-to-date as possible.

Of critical importance in evaluating a biographical source is the accuracy of the information provided. Basically, there are two sources of this information: the biographies themselves and information provided or written about individuals (secondary sources). While biographies are certainly capable of providing accurate information, authors may omit facts regarded as unfavorable. Retrospective biographical sources must rely on secondary sources for the information. These sources may have incorrect or biased information, depending on the author. To verify questionable information, consult other resources.

Typically, the criteria for inclusion in a specific biographical source are provided in prefatory material. However, how those criteria are defined and applied determines how comprehensive the source is. Attempt to locate as many individuals as possible who meet the criteria, as this increases the value of the resource. Often the criteria are stated in general terms and, hence, are difficult to determine. Regardless of the criteria used, the source's scope and criterion should be in agreement.

When evaluating biographical sources, as with all other reference tools, ease of use is a critical factor. If the source is poorly organized, or if the indexes or cross-references are inadequate, the information desired may never be located. Obviously, electronic sources offer a definite advantage over print materials concerning ease of use. Electronic retrieval (CD-ROM, online) allows students to retrieve biographical entries for individuals with common characteristics, such as date of birth, occupation, and so forth. Electronic searching also permits students to simultaneously search entries from numerous different printed editions or volumes of a specific biographical tool. Information, regardless of format, should be presented in a concise, organized, and straightforward fashion.

Currency is also an important factor when evaluating biographical sources.

Out-of-date information can lead to inaccuracies regarding an individual's address, current profession, etc. Comparing entries for the same person in varying biographical sources may assist in revealing errors. Publication frequency is another issue in maintaining current information about biographies. Biographical directories are typically revised every year or two. However, the electronic versions of these sources are often updated only when a new print edition is prepared; therefore, they may be no more current than the print sources. Biographical dictionaries are revised less frequently. However, dictionaries that are published serially, such as *Current Biography*, often publish new or revised entries on prominent people whose earlier entries are out of date.

In selecting and evaluating biographical sources, tools and aids are available to assist school library media specialists. Many of the review journals (as described in chapter two) contain separate sections regarding reference sources. These tools should be used to identify the most suitable biographical sources for your school situation. In addition, as with other reference resources, elicit the assistance of faculty members, experts in the field.

Dealing as much with individual ego and pride as with accomplishment and fact, early biographical reference sources were great sources of income for what some call the tin cup brigades. These were people who literally moved into a community, established a biographical book of that community, and then charged individuals for an entry. These mug books are a far cry from the legitimate works. Yet, ironically enough, historians are grateful for the information they provide of America. Even today, vanity biographical schemes abound.

Basic Sources

There are numerous biographical reference sources available on every imaginable significant person and in every format. The focus of this section, however, is biographical sources appropriate for use in school library media centers. The sources appropriate for your school library media center will depend on your situation—the school, students, and community, as well as budget and personal preferences. The biographical sources mentioned are commonly used; they are not all-inclusive, but merely examples that are suitable for school library media centers. Further information about specific biographical sources is presented in journals and other selection and evaluation tools (as explained in chapter two).

WHO'S WHO

Who's Who in America, (print format), a three-volume set by Marquis Who's Who Reed Reference Publishing, is a current biographical directory that is a useful source for many school library media centers. This biographical source, published biennially and arranged alphabetically, includes individuals for their achievements and contributions to society. Inclusion is not based simply on wealth or notoriety. The information about individuals is obtained from the biography, if possible. *Who's Who in America* is used primarily to locate basic information about individuals such as date of birth, positions held, address, degrees earned, and the like. This source is usually the first source to consult when a student requests basic biographical data on a prominent American. Who's Who publishes four United States regional directories:

East, Midwest, West, and South/Southwest (Marquis Who's Who Reed Reference Publishing). Canada and Mexico are included in each regional Who's Who. Several topical Who's Who are also published on topics such as entertainment, religion, etc. Examples of other Who's Who include *Who's Who among Black Americans* (Gale Reference Publishing), *Who's Who in Media and Communications* (Marquis Who's Who Reed Reference Publishing), *Who's Who among Hispanic Americans* (Gale Reference Publishing), and numerous others. Illustrations of specialized Who's Who include *Who's Who in American Art* (print format published biennially) and *Who's Who in American Politics* (print format published every two years) by Marquis Who's Who. Who's Who is also international in scope. Two examples are *Who's Who in the World*, published every two years by Marquis Who's Who Reed Reference Publishing and *The International Who's Who*, published annually by Gale Research Publishing.

CURRENT BIOGRAPHICAL DICTIONARIES

Current Biography (H. W. Wilson, print format published monthly except December; CD-ROM published annually; online (fee-based) at www.hwwilson.com/databases/cbcdrom.htm) is one of the most recognized current biographical dictionaries. *Current Biography* provides objective and carefully researched biographical essays about persons in a wide range of fields, persons prominent in their disciplines. The essays are primarily based on articles that have appeared in magazines and newspapers. Each essay includes a photograph of the subject and a list of sources upon which the essay is based. It provides a life history of the individual without reading a full biography. Each issue of *Current Biography* contains approximately 15 essays; at the end of each year, the essays from the monthly issues are cumulated in the *Current Biography Yearbook*. A widely used biographical source for middle and high schools is *Biography Today*. This source is published annually by Omnigraphics in three softbound issues and one bound, cumulative volume. Each issue of *Biography Today* contains entries for approximately 20 people, judged to be of interest to young adults. An extremely valuable online biographical source is www.biography.com. This resource offers more than 20,000 personalities and 2,400 videos for the user to search. Biography.com also features Born on This Day, Top 10 Biographies, Biographies on Arts and Entertainment, Features, Biography Book Club, and numerous other useful biographical elements.

AUTHOR SOURCES AND LITERARY CRITICISM

Print Resources

- *American Indian Autobiography* (University of California Press)
- *American Indian Literature: An Anthology* (University of Oklahoma Press)
- *A Bibliography of Native American Writers 1772-1924* (Scarecrow Press)
- *Biographical Dictionary of Indians of the Americas* (American Indian Publishing, Inc.)
- *Blue Dawn, Red Earth: New Native American Storytellers* (Doubleday)
- *Dictionary of Native American Literature* (Garland Publishing, Inc.)
- *Harper's Anthology of 20th Century Native American Poetry* (Harper & Row)
- *Home Places: Contemporary Native American Writings* (University of Arizona Press)
- *Literature By and About the American Indian: An Annotated Bibliography*
- (Illinois National Council of Teachers of English)
- *Literature of the American Indian: Views and Interpretations. A Gathering of Indian Memories, Symbolic Contexts and Literary Criticism* (New American Libraries)
- *Native American Literature* (Twayne Publishers)
- *Native American Literature: A Brief Introduction and Anthology* (HarperCollins College Publishers)
- *Native American Women: A Biographical Dictionary* (Garland Publishing)
- *Native Americans Autobiography: An Anthology* (University of Wisconsin Press)
- *Native Americans: Portrait of the Peoples* (Visible Ink Press)
- *Returning the Gift: Poetry and Prose from the First North American Native Winter's Festival* (University of Arizona Press)
- *Who Was When in Native American History: Indians and Non-Indians from Early Contacts Through 1900* (Facts on File)

Author sources is one significant area in many school media reference collections. Students study and learn about the lives of authors as a part of the curriculum. The library media center can supplement these studies with visiting authors and other similar activities. The following are examples of author sources appropriate for school library media centers. *Contemporary Authors*, published by Gale Reference Publishing (print format is updated annually; CD-ROM format semiannually), is a current biographical dictionary. This source includes not only authors of books, but also journalists, musicians, etc. Another similar biographical source is, *Something about the Author* (Gale Reference Publishing). Several volumes are published each year and each volume contains a cumulative index to the entire set, which includes authors and illustrators of works created for children and young adults. *World Authors* (H. W. Wilson, updated periodically) is yet another well-known series on authors. This international source includes not only essential biographical information, but also bibliographies or works by and about the author. Entries are nearly 1,000 words, with a picture of the author and a listing of published works. There are also numerous online sources regarding authors and literary criticism such as The Reference Center at the Internet Public Library (www.ipl.org/ref) and The Children's Literature Web Guide (www.acs.ucalgary.ca/~dkbrown). These two resources offer excellent author information as well as sections on literary criticism.

Retrospective Biographical Dictionaries

Retrospective biographical dictionaries differ from current dictionaries in that they typically include only individuals who are not living. A major biographical source of this type for school library media centers is the *McGraw-Hill Encyclopedia of World Biography* (McGraw-Hill). This source was compiled specifically for students in secondary schools. The selection of names is made with curriculum needs in mind. The names included are chosen by conventional standards of importance or familiarity; however, living persons are occasionally included. *McGraw-Hill Encyclopedia of World Biography* is composed of 11 volumes of text and a 12th volume consisting of an index and study guides. An authority in the field with whom the biography is associated writes each entry; portraits are included. The study guides located in volume 12 allow one to develop a list of individuals who were associated with significant events, eras, or historical trends. The biographical essays assist students in locating further sources of information. The dates and facts are, for the most part, accurate because the authors of each essay have been selected for their expertise in the field. For ready-reference purposes *Webster's New Biographical Dictionary* (G & C Merriam Company) offers brief information, but a more comprehensive coverage. This biographical source provides short, one-paragraph descriptions of the important contributions of approximately 30,000 individuals from the past. *The Dictionary of American Biography* (Charles Scribner's Sons) is an excellent source for extensive biographical information about prominent deceased Americans. There are more than 18,000 entries in the *Dictionary of American Biography*; they are arranged alphabetically by surname. The entries, written by scholars, are entirely in essay format and vary from a couple of paragraphs to several pages (a few as long a 10 pages). Equally useful is the *American National Biography*, found online at (www.anb.org/aboutanb.html). *The Concise Dictionary of American Biography* (Charles Scribner's Sons) is a one-volume work that provides brief entries for each individual. Some entries offer only basic facts, while more important figures have short essays about the individual. Another important retrospective source is *Who Was Who in America* (Marquis Who's Who Reed Reference Publishing). This source provides basic factual data about deceased prominent Americans; it is revised every four to five years.

Indirect biographical sources tell where information about individuals may be found rather than providing the information directly. An indirect source is the best place to start a search for information about a person if the student requests a number of different sources. *Biography Index* (H. W. Wilson) offers references to biographical articles in nearly 3,000 periodicals and to approximately 2,000 book-length individual and collective biographies. This resource is available in print format, online, and on CD-ROM. The print format is published quarterly with annual and biennial accumulations and the CD-ROM format is revised quarterly.

Conclusion

School library media specialists have a massive number of biographical sources from which to choose. The purpose of this chapter is to introduce you to types of biographical sources and to provide useful examples within each type. Each school library media center will require different sources depending on the unique situation surrounding it. Not only are there a wide variety of biographical sources, both individual and collective, but resources now aslo come in a selection of formats as well. Additionally, it should not be overlooked that biographical information can be found in other reference sources, such as encyclopedias. The search strategy employed will depend on the type and amount of biographical information requested. As with the majority of reference questions, the first step is to obtain as much information as possible from the student. Can the question be answered by searching one source (ready-reference) or do a variety of sources need to be consulted (research)? Regardless of the question, it can only be answered if the proper biographical sources are available and correctly applied in your school library media center.

Webliography and Additional Examples of Online Biographical Resources

American Academy of Achievement
    www.achievement.org
    This Web site provides biographies of high achievers in the arts, business, public service, science and exploration, sports, etc.

*American National Biography (ANB) Online
    www.anb.org/aboutanb.html
    This site provides the latest update of the American National Biography Online, which comprises 24 articles, including ones on recently deceased notables and intriguing figures from the 17th and 18th centuries.

*American Presidents: Life Portraits
    www.americanpresidents.org
    This site contains a complete video archive of all American Presidents: Life Portraits programming, plus these additional resources: Biographical facts, Key events of each presidency, Presidential places, and Reference material.

*Biography.com
    www.biography.com/search
    This online resource searches more than 25,000 of the greatest lives—past and present.

Biography Dictionary
> http://www.s9.com/biography
> *This site includes nearly 30,000 notable men and women who have shaped our world from ancient times to present day. One can search by name, year, profession, literary or artistic work, achievement, and much more.*

*Children's Literature Web Guide
> www.acs.ucalgary.ca/~dkbrown
> *This Web site includes Features, Discussion Boards, Quick Reference, and many more links (Authors on the Web, Stories on the Web, and so forth).*

*Contemporary Authors
> http://contemporarylit.about.com/cs/authors/
> *From Abbey to Yen Mah. From Le Carré to LeGuin. From Barry to Barry... there are thousands of authors to consider and new profiles added daily via this site.*

*Current Biography
> www.hwwilson.com/databases/cbcdrom.htm
> *This Web site reflects the entire contents of the printed monthly* Current Biography; *it contains reliable information about people making tomorrow's headlines, plus historical figures back to World War II.*

Dead People Server
> www.deadpeople.info
> *This is a database of interesting celebrities who are long dead or newly dead. (An unconventional site!)*

Distinguished Women of the Past and Present
> www.distinguishedwomen.com
> *This Web site offers biographies of women who contributed to their fields in different ways, including writers, educators, scientists, heads of state, politicians, artists, entertainers, and so on.*

Infoplease.com/People
> www.infoplease.com/people.html__
> *The Infoplease biography search page contains data from* The Columbia Encyclopedia, The Infoplease Dictionary *and* Information Please Almanac— *extremely useful!*

Lives, The Biography Resource
> http://amillionlives.com
> *This site is the largest guide to post-human biography on the Web (people who have died); it provides links to biographies, autobiographies, memoirs, diaries, letters, narratives, oral histories, and resources on biographical criticism and special collections.*

*Reference Center at the Internet Public Library
   www.ipl.org
   This site provides the biographies section of IP—including such subheadings as, Artists and Architects, Authors, Entertainers, Musicians and Composers, Politicians and Rulers, and Scientists and Inventors.

Thinkers 50
   www.thinkers50.co.uk
   This Web site ranks the top 50 business thinkers of all time and includes biographical information.

* denotes Web sites noted within this chapter

Chapter 6

Dictionaries and Encyclopedias

One might ask, "Do dictionaries and encyclopedias still matter today?" You bet! More dictionaries and encyclopedias are available—in an amazing range of topics, print and nonprint—than ever before! Remember that there is such a thing as an intellectual division of labor—not only among people, but also among types of books and reference materials. Sometimes a dictionary or encyclopedia is precisely what is required, regardless of format. How fortunate our students are to have access to thousands of dictionaries and encyclopedias, to meet the needs of every student in every imaginable situation.

Dictionaries indicate spelling, meaning, pronunciation, and syllabication of words. General encyclopedias capsulate and organize the world's accumulated knowledge. This chapter discusses types of dictionaries and encyclopedias appropriate for school library media situations (print, electronic, and online), as well as selection and evaluation of these vital reference sources.

DICTIONARIES

Introduction

Dictionaries are primarily thought of as a means of verifying spelling and defining words. Dictionaries are of two basic types and can be defined as: 1) a reference resource containing words usually arranged along with information about their forms, pronunciations, functions, etymologies, meanings, and syntactical and idiomatic uses; and 2) a reference source alphabetically listing terms or names important to a particular subject or activity, along with discussion of their meanings and applications. Dictionaries may either be descriptive (how the language is actually used) or prescriptive (how it ought to be used). The descriptive philosophy claims that language is ever changing and that dictionaries should reflect those changes. Believers of the descriptive viewpoint realize that few rules are absolute; different societal and cultural situations offer their own rules. The prescriptive view claims that the major role of dictionaries is to set standards, support traditional usage, and prevent corruption of language by jargon and slang. Most of the Merriam-Webster dictionaries take the stance that "almost anything goes" as long as it is popular. For example, did you know that "ASAP" is currently a real word in the dictionary? At the other end of the spectrum are dictionaries that provide absolute rules of usage, such as *Webster's New World Dictionary*. Somewhere in-between descriptive and prescriptive dictionaries are the more practical types, such as *The American Heritage Dictionary*.

Two categories of dictionaries are unabridged and abridged. An unabridged dictionary attempts to include all of the words in the language that are in use at the time the dictionary is assembled. Unabridged dictionaries contain more than 265,000 words. Abridged dictionaries are selectively compiled and typically based on a larger dictionary. They are created for a certain level of student use. Most dictionaries are abridged. Types of dictionaries other than English language include foreign language, historical, geographical, biographical, slang and dialect, thesauri, subject, visual, and so forth.

Evaluation and Selection

Evaluation of Dictionaries

AUTHORITY:
- A reputable publisher is important (print and electronic)
    Examples of reputable publishers include:
        Merriam-Webster
        Random House
        Scott Foresman
        Houghton Mifflin
        Macmillan
        Simon & Schuster
        Oxford University Press

FORMAT:
- Consider binding, arrangement of words, and readability.
- Note the effectiveness of purpose as stated in the title or introduction.

CURRENCY:
- Dictionary revision is never ending; a major advantage of electronic dictionaries is rapid update.

ACCURACY:
- Spelling and definition should be precise.
- Words should be modernized.
- Meanings should be precise and clearly indicated.
- Definitions should be understandable and unambiguous.

Remember, above all else, that no dictionary is perfect; language is continually evolving (remember "ASAP"?). Each dictionary has its good features and its defects. Basically, dictionaries are written for a specific audience, such as high school students, or for a particular purpose. In evaluating dictionaries, it is critical to determine the degree to which a dictionary has succeeded in fulfilling the purpose of the population addressed. These are exceptionally critical elements for school library media specialists, as unique populations are served via dictionaries. The following criteria should be considered when evaluating dictionaries for school library media centers: authority, format, currency, and accuracy.

The authority or reputation of the publisher is an essential factor in judging the quality of dictionaries because staffs, rather than individuals, normally compile them. As with other reference areas, there are reputable publishers for general dictionaries, as well. The larger, better-known publishers in North America include Merriam-Webster; Random House; Scott Foresman; Houghton Mifflin; Macmillan; Simon and Schuster; and Oxford University Press. Additional reputable publishers exist for specialized dictionaries. Reputation of the publisher remains a vital factor in electronic versions as well. The same publishers as the print versions create many electronic dictionaries.

Major format considerations for dictionaries include binding, arrangement of words, and readability. School library media centers should have a minimum of one print unabridged, hardcover dictionary that will withstand frequent use. Readability is a particularly important consideration for school library media centers. Is the print size large enough; is boldface type used effectively; is it clear and user-friendly? Dictionaries should be judged on their effectiveness of purpose as stated in the title, purpose, or introduction, regardless of format. For example, an elementary level dictionary should include words likely to be used in reading and writing by an elementary student. The major advantages of dictionaries in electronic format are multiple access points and time saved by searching, as well as the numerous types offered via the Internet. When a dictionary is Web-based, a school library media specialist should ask all of the customary questions regarding its relative value to a printed version. It is also important, however, to consider other variables that relate to Internet resources, such as graphics, links, maneuverability, and so on.

Currency is yet another important factor to consider when evaluating dictionaries. Dictionary revision is never-ending. New words, revised definitions of older words with new meanings, and deletions and additions of technical and popular terms are continually occurring. An obvious advantage of Web-based dictionaries is rapid updates. Be aware, however, that just because a dictionary is on the Internet does not necessarily mean that it is more current than the print equivalent.

In determining the accuracy of dictionaries, two basic considerations are spelling and definition. Where there are several forms of spelling, they should be clearly indicated. Frequently, two different spellings are provided, and both are acceptable. One should check words that have been modernized. Dictionaries typically provide the modern meaning of words first. Meanings should be precise, separate and distinct, as well as clearly indicated. Definitions should reflect the meaning(s) of words in understandable, unambiguous terms. Illustrative examples or quotations from literature can assist in defining words in context.

The selection of dictionaries, as well as other reference materials, should be based on the particular needs and requirements of the school, student population, and community served. Additional elements to consider include the age and condition of print dictionaries currently in the school media center collection, along with budget. The long, useful life of a large, unabridged print dictionary will typically justify the cost. Become aware, however, of the plethora of wide-ranging dictionaries available via the Internet. Also, remain alert to dictionaries geared specifically for school library media centers. It should be noted that college level dictionaries might be valuable in high school library media centers, particularly for advanced students. One little known, generally misunderstood belief is that there is no copyright on the use of the word Webster; this word is common property and can be used by any publisher. When selecting dictionaries, it is advisable to read reviews and stick with standard titles or publishers. Several selection tools are available for dictionaries, such as *Kister's Best Dictionaries for Adults and Young People: A Comparative* Guide (Oryx Press) and reviews provided in *Booklist* (American Library Association).

Basic Sources

ENGLISH LANGUAGE DICTIONARIES

Probably the most notable unabridged dictionary of the English language is *Webster's Third New International* (Merriam-Webster, Inc., 2002). This large, comprehensive dictionary includes such items as the date when a word or phrase first entered the language and identification of vocabulary specifically of the American origin. Random House offers an unabridged dictionary in CD-ROM format, entitled the *Random House Unabridged Electronic Dictionary*. This current, descriptive-style dictionary includes more than 300,000 entries and 2,500 illustrations.

Numerous abridged dictionaries exist that are appropriate for school library media centers. *Merriam-Webster's Collegiate Dictionary* (print format) represents an extensive revision and updating in both the entries and special sections. Each entry includes the part of speech, pronunciation, inflections, etymology, definitions, and notes on usage and synonymy. Definitions in this dictionary are precise and clear. Another useful abridged dictionary in print format is *The Concise American Heritage Dictionary*, which is the abridged version of *The American Heritage Dictionary of the English Language* (Houghton Mifflin, 2000). This dictionary is particularly appropriate for high school students. It is easy to read and the typeface and illustrations are large and clear. *The Concise American Heritage Dictionary* is extremely complete for a condensed edition. Other suitable abridged dictionaries in print format are *Webster's New World Dictionary of the American Language* (Prentice-Hall) and *The Random House Webster's College Dictionary* (Random House).

For elementary age students, the following abridged dictionaries in print format are appropriate: *American Heritage First Dictionary* (Houghton Mifflin*); Macmillan First Dictionary* (Simon & Schuster); *Scott Foresman Beginning Dictionary* (Scott Foresman); *Longman Elementary Dictionary* (Addison Wesley Longman); *Webster's Elementary Dictionary* (Merriam-Webster); *Thorndike-Barnhart Children's Dictionary* (Addison Wesley); *Webster's New World Children's Dictionary* (Macmillan); and the *American Heritage Children's Dictionary* (Houghton Mifflin). I am particularly fond of the last three dictionaries mentioned above. *Thorndike-Barnhart Children's Dictionary* provides information regarding how to use the dictionary, as well as synonym studies and word source sections. It includes more than 25,000 words, 800 study pages, and more than 1,000 color photographs and other artwork. *Webster's New World Children's Dictionary* includes a CD-ROM with word learning games and an electronic dictionary. It offers colorful illustrations, as well as a comprehensive thesaurus and reference section. *The American Heritage Children's Dictionary* is approximately 1,000 pages in length and features a four-page thesaurus, a 10-page section on phonics and spelling, as well as a reference section, synonyms, building vocabulary, and world histories.

The following are reputable electronic dictionaries; they vary slightly in arrangement, format, and length of definitions: *The Random House Webster's Dictionary and Thesaurus College Edition* (Random House) and *The American Heritage Talking Dictionary* (Houghton Mifflin). For elementary school students, *The World Book Dictionary* and *Macmillan Dictionary for Children* (both CD-ROM format) are reliable choices.

Numerous online dictionaries exist, such as: Your Dictionary.com (www.yourdictionary.com); OneLook (www.onelook.com); Cambridge Dictionaries Online (www.dictionary.cambridge.org); Dictionary.com (http://dictionary.reference .com); Encarta (http://encarta.msn.com/encnet/features/dictionary/dictionaryhome .aspx); Merriam-Webster Online (www.m-w.com); Wordsmyth (www.wordsmyth.net); Bartleby.com (www.bartleby.com/61/s0.html); Infoplease (www.infoplease.com/ dictionary.html); Wikipedia (http://en.wikipedia.org/wiki/Main_Page); AskOxford (www.askoxford.com); and iTools (www.itools.com/lang/). Don't overlook these free resources!

FOREIGN LANGUAGE DICTIONARIES

A student who simply seeks a common foreign word or phrase is likely to find the answer in almost any general dictionary. However, when it comes to more complicated, specialized words, students should refer to a bilingual dictionary. There are several reputable publishers of foreign language dictionaries including Cassell, HarperCollins, Charles Scribner's Sons, Simon and Schuster, and Oxford University Press. These dictionaries all provide similar information, including pronunciations, definitions, slang words, colloquialisms, and idioms. Foreign language dictionaries are essential resources for school library media centers. The types and number of foreign language dictionaries purchased will, of course, depend on the school's curriculum and student body. Examples of online foreign language sources include Word2Word.com (www.word2word.com/dictionary.html); Dictionaries by Language (http://dir.yahoo.com/Reference/Dictionaries/Language); Your Free Language Wizard (www.foreignword.com); iLoveLanguages (www.ilovelanguages.com); and Glossaries by Languages (www.lai.com/glossaries.html).

HISTORICAL DICTIONARIES

The Oxford English Dictionary (Oxford University Press, second edition), print and electronic formats, is a scholarly compilation (print is 22 volumes) including extensive etymologies that record the history of words and meanings in use since 1150. The purpose of this dictionary is to trace the history of the English language. *The Oxford English Dictionary* in electronic format (fee-based) contains definitions for most of the words in the English language and, in addition, information regarding their origins and quotations showing their range of meanings from the time they entered the language to present. *The New Shorter Oxford English Dictionary* (print format) is a current, two-volume historical dictionary. This dictionary includes more than 500,000 words and 80,000 quotations. *The New Shorter* is moderately priced and an excellent resource for etymologies and learning the fine points of history. The single volume *Barnhart Dictionary of Etymology* (H. W. Wilson) is yet another historical dictionary. An excellent feature of this dictionary is that it emphasizes the way language is written and spoken in the United States today.

SLANG AND DIALECT DICTIONARIES

Does a school library media center need dictionaries on slang and dialect? This question is debatable and depends on the particular school and community served. However, slang and dialect dictionaries are useful for indicating the variations of meaning given slang words as well as providing expressions that are not well defined in an ordinary dictionary. The most notable slang and dialect dictionaries include*: The Oxford Dictionary of Modern Slang* (Oxford University Press); *The Thesaurus of Slang* (Facts on File); *Random House Historical Dictionary of American Slang* (Random House), *and Dictionary of American Regional English* (Harvard University Press). An example of an online slang dictionary is A Dictionary of Slang (http://www.peevish.co.uk/slang). Always be cautious regarding the nature of the language included.

THESAURI

A thesaurus is a specialized dictionary that deals solely with word synonyms and antonyms. The best-known thesauri are based on the work of Peter Mark Roget. It should be noted, as with the word "Webster's," "Roget's" cannot be copyrighted and is free to any publisher. The most notable Roget's thesaurus is the *Roget's International Thesaurus* (HarperCollins, print format). Two additional Roget's print formats that are valuable for school library media center collections are *Roget's A to Z* and *Roget's II: The New Thesaurus* (HarperCollins). Thesauri are also available on CD-ROM (as well as online via word processing programs). Two thesauri in CD-ROM format include *Roget's II: Electronic Thesaurus* (Houghton Mifflin) and *Merriam-Webster's Collegiate Thesaurus* (Merriam-Webster). Both contain more than 70,000 entries and have the advantage of rapid, easy searching. Random House also offers a combination of thesaurus and dictionary in CD-ROM format, *Random House Webster's Dictionary and Thesaurus College Edition*. Numerous thesauri are available online, typically accompanying a variety of dictionaries. Two interesting Web sites to view regarding thesauri are http://dmoz.org/Reference/Thesauri and http://hilt.cdlr.strath.ac.uk/Sources/thesauri.html.

SPECIALTY DICTIONARIES

Specialty dictionaries explain meanings of specific words in terms of professions, occupations, or areas of interest. When selecting specialty dictionaries, it is important to determine that there is no other resource currently in the collection that provides the same or remarkably similar information. One should look for purposeful illustrations, clear and thorough definitions, and current terminology in specialty dictionaries. There is an enormity of specialty dictionaries available dealing with every imaginable area of interest. The following resources are examples of the wide variety of specialty dictionaries available in print format that are appropriate for school library media centers: *A Dictionary of Battles* (Wordsworth Editions Ltd.); *Dictionary of Classical Mythology* (Cassell Academic); *Harvard Dictionary of Music* (Belknap Press); *A Dictionary of Media Terms* (Fitzroy Dearborn Publishing); *A Dictionary of Geography* (Oxford University Press); *Dictionary of Science and Technology* (Academic Press); *A Consumer's Dictionary of Food Additives* (Three Rivers Press); *Dictionary of Fictional Characters* (Writer Publishing); *Concise Dictionary of the Opera* (Oxford University Press); *The Civil War Dictionary* (Vintage Books/Random House); *The New Dictionary of American Family Names* (New American Library); and *The Illustrated Computer Dictionary for Dummies* (IDG Books Worldwide). Topics of specialty dictionaries range from Accounting to Wine, and everything in-between. Two examples of online specialty dictionaries are A Basic Dictionary of ASL (American Sign Language) Terms (www.masterstech-home.com/ASLDict.html) and Strange and Unusual Dictionaries (www.blueray.com/dictionary/).

    With dictionaries now available on most word processing software, the focus of general dictionaries has altered. Many features common to general dictionaries are provided on word processing programs (spelling, synonyms, etc.). These elements provide easy and rapid access to basic dictionary functions. However, dictionaries provide much more than the basic word processing features. In addition, a dictionary is often required when one is not working at a computer. Therefore, there still remains a distinct and important place for numerous versions of general, foreign language, historical, slang and dialect, thesauri, and specialty dictionaries in today's modern, technological school library media centers.

Webliography

AskOxford

> www.askoxford.com
> *This Web site includes such features as Ask the Experts, Better Writing, World of Words, Word of the Day, Quote of the Day, and much more.*

A Basic Dictionary of ASL (American Sign Language) Terms

> www.masterstech-home.com/ASLDict.html
> *This site offers both animated and text definitions. The text definitions also include letter or number sign images to aid in visualizing the sign.*

Cambridge Dictionaries Online

> www.dictionary.cambridge.org
> *This online dictionary ranges from intermediate to proficiency level; it is clear, up-to-date, and easy to use.*

Dictionaries by Language

> http://dir.yahoo.com/Reference/Dictionaries/Language
> *This Web site includes everything from American Sign Language to Yiddish!*

Dictionary.com

> http://dictionary.reference.com
> *This site includes such features as Bookstore, Fun and Games, Language Resources, Thesurus.com, Tools, Translation, and Word of the Day.*

A Dictionary of Slang

> www.peevish.u-net.com/slang/
> *This is an online dictionary of slang, with new slang added every month!*

Encarta

> http://encarta.msn.com/encnet/features/dictionary/dictionaryhome.aspx
> *This useful Web site encourages learning and respects the role of parents in their children's education.*

Glossaries by Languages
www.lai.com/glossaries.html
This is an extremely comprehensive site, including languages from Arabic to Gaelic to Welsh.

iLoveLanguages
www.ilovelanguages.com
This Web site is a comprehensive catalog of language-related Internet resources. The more than 2,000 links at iLoveLanguages have been hand-reviewed.

iTools
www.itools.com/lang/
Via this site, one can learn the meaning of any word, its correct spelling, how to pronounce it, and where it originated.

Medline Plus
www.nlm.nih.gov/medlineplus/mplusdictionary.html
This Web site is a gold mine of good health information from the world's largest medical library, the National Library of Medicine.

Merriam-Webster Online
www.m-w.com
This online source includes Merriam-Webster's Real Time Words, which consist of unedited entries randomly selected from millions of searches on Merriam-Webster Online that make the Top Ten List of the most frequently looked-up words.

OneLook
www.onelook.com
This Web site offers 6,002,182 words in 966 dictionaries, indexed!

Strange and Unusual Dictionaries
www.blueray.com/dictionary/
This site offers unusual dictionaries, such as The White Queens Dictionary of One-Letter Words, Dictionary of All-Consonant Words, and Dictionary of All-Vowel Words.

Thesauri
http://hilt.cdlr.strath.ac.uk/Sources/thesauri.html
A very comprehensive source, beginning with "Access to Asian Vegetables Thesaurus!"

Thesauri
>   http://dmoz.org/Reference/Thesauri
>   *This site is the largest, most comprehensive human-edited directory on the Web. It is constructed and maintained by a vast, global community of volunteer editors.*

Wikipedia
>   http://en.wikipedia.org/wiki/Main_Page
>   *This Web site offers more than 300,000 portals of information!*

Wordsmyth
>   www.wordsmyth.net
>   *This online source provides useful, accessible reference resources and is made expressly for elementary school-aged children.*

Word2Word.com
>   www.word2word.com/dictionary.html
>   *This site provides links in the hope of developing a better understanding of others through the use of language; it offers numerous online dictionaries.*

Your Dictionary.com
>   www.yourdictionary.com
>   *This Web site uses the database of* The American Heritage® Dictionary of the English Language *(AHD), published by Houghton-Mifflin Company, as well as* Roget's Thesaurus.

Your Free Language Wizard
>   www.foreignword.com
>   *This online source provides access to more than 200 online dictionaries for 70 languages.*

Chapter *7*

Geographical Sources

Introduction

Geographical reference sources can be thought of as works of art. They provide aesthetic satisfaction and the opportunity to let one's imagination wander. These reference materials are used primarily to answer location questions. Geographical sources may be used at an uncomplicated level (for example, Where is the country of Oman located?) or at a more sophisticated level involving relationships regarding environment, history, climate, and political boundaries (for example, How has the melting of the polar ice caps affected the climate in the Northern Hemisphere?). Human society has become more global than ever before, therefore, recent geographical resources are a necessity. When a student requests the identification of a geographic place, normally the answer can be found in an atlas or an individual map. Some questions may require extremely up-to-date geographical materials—atlases, maps, and other resources should be specifically selected for current event-type questions. Responding to the need for current information may require the use of online resources. Another category of geographical questions includes historical ones. Information of this nature can be located in older atlases and related geographical sources. Therefore, age need not be a primary criterion when weeding geographical materials. Geographical requests can vary widely, requiring an assortment of geography-related sources such as current, historical and thematic atlases, maps of varying types, gazetteers, travel guides, and even general reference materials that include geographic information such as encyclopedias. With the wealth of geographical sources currently online and on CD-ROMs and DVDs, it is now significantly less complicated to fulfill the diverse requests required by students. The categories of geographical sources considered in this chapter include print and electronic: maps, atlases, and gazetteers, and other general geographical sources appropriate for school library media centers.

Maps are representations of certain boundaries on a flat surface. However, there are a wide variety of maps designed for every purpose, from indicating soil content to determining the vegetation in a particular city via satellite imaging. A physical map traces the different features of the land from rivers and valleys to mountains and hills. A street (route) map shows roads, railroads, bridges, and similar phenomena. A map depicting specific conditions is typically referred to as a thematic map. These, either separately or as one, make up a large number of maps found in atlases. An atlas is simply a volume of maps. Atlases can provide, at a nominal cost, maps of the whole world in one book. Individual atlases include numerous subjects and offer reference information on geographical features, oceans, space, and historical and political geography of particular areas. Atlases may be divided into three categories: current, historical, and thematic. Gazetteers or geographic dictionaries provide information regarding geographic place-names. Often they include information on such topics as population, climate, and economy. Electronic geographic sources are becoming a vitally important part of school library media reference resources. These sources serve a multitude of valuable functions, are typically user-friendly, and are remarkably current. Often electronic and print geographic materials complement each other; this chapter will discuss all formats of geographic resources.

Evaluation and Selection

Evaluation of Geographic Sources

PUBLISHER (AUTHORITY):
- It is best to purchase from a reputable publisher of geographic materials.
- If the publisher is unknown, determine other works it may have published.

SCALE:
- Understand that scale is the most important element, as it defines the amount of information that can be shown.
- The scale should be clearly defined and appropriate for the intended audience.

CURRENCY:
- Our geographic world is changing rapidly!
- A five-year-old atlas is considered historical.

INDEXING:
- An effective geographical index is an alphabetical list of all place-names that appear on the map.
- A comprehensive index is important.
- Electronic geographical sources should provide rapid and user-friendly access to information.

FORMAT:
- Regardless of the format, the resources must provide the desired information quickly and easily; be clear and legible.

Geographic sources may be evaluated using many of the same criteria as other reference sources; however, there are several additional points to consider. Because these materials depend on graphic arts and mathematics as well, further issues should be noted regarding evaluation and selection. The basic criteria to be considered when evaluating geographic resources include publisher (authority), scale, currency, indexing, and format.

As with any reference area, there exist competent and reputable publishers in the field. This is also true of geographic sources. In the United States, the leading publishers include Rand McNally, C. S. Hammond, and the National Geographic Society. Prominent international publishers include John Bartholomew and Oxford University Press. When the publisher's reputation is unknown, it is best to determine other works it may have published. This is particularly important when considering electronic geographic sources, where the vendor or publisher may differ from standard companies. Numerous smaller firms also produce geographic materials, in particular, city maps. In all cases it is best to purchase resources from reliable publishers or locally reputable organizations. It should also be noted that geography is a component of numerous other reference materials such as encyclopedias and almanacs. It is important that the publisher of the encyclopedia, etc. has a reliable reputation as well.

Scale is a characteristic that makes geographic resources different from other reference materials. Maps are usually classed according to scales. They must be drawn to scale such that accurate comparisons may be distinguished between a verbal scale and a representative fraction. One unit on a map equals a particular number of units on the ground (for example, one inch equals 10 miles). Scale is the most important element of a map, as it defines the amount of information that can be shown, as well as the size of the geographic area. The scale from map to map in a given atlas may vary widely, although better atlases attempt to standardize their work. An effective map or atlas identifies the scale; as a school library media specialist it is important that you decide the appropriate scale for your student population.

Another essential criterion for geographic resources is currency. Because the world is changing so rapidly, it is of utmost importance that the school library media center provides up-to-date geographical information. School library media specialists should update their world maps frequently, although electronic formats are now supplying current information on a regular basis. A world atlas that is five years old portrays enough obsolete information to be considered only for historical purposes. A multitude of changes occurs on a continual basis regarding geographical sources—place-names, boundaries, roads, etc. Revisions of maps and atlases (completely overhauled and developed) normally take place every 10 years—the span of time between the American census.

An effective geographical index is an alphabetical list of all place-names that appear on the map. A comprehensive index is as important in geographic reference works as the maps themselves. In addition, there should be a reference to the exact map as well as latitude, longitude, and grid information. Indexes may also include such items as national parks, mountains, and historical sites. An effective atlas or map indexes as many features as possible. Online and electronic software should provide rapid and user-friendly access to the information it includes.

Geographic sources in any format should provide the desired information as quickly and easily as possible; it must be clear and legible. Maps with fewer items of information are typically easier to read; the actual number of points represented on a map is a major editorial decision. Electronic geographical sources are growing increasingly important and necessary. There are numerous high quality and user-friendly electronic materials. National Geographic's online site (www.nationalgeographic.com/maps/index.html) is an excellent source, offering Dynamic Maps, Atlas Maps, Flags and Facts, satellite imaging, and many other useful features. Rand McNally's online site (www.randmcnally.com) is also a valuable source for planning trips, exploring maps, and finding addresses, and driving directions. The format of geographical sources should be selected on the basis of student needs and abilities, as well as relative cost.

As with the selection of all reference materials, each school library media specialist must determine the informational requirements and desires of the school, student population, and community served. This is also true of the appropriate selection and evaluation of geographical materials. However, locating suitable selection tools and aids in this field is more difficult than other reference areas. Several journals provide reviews of geographical sources (some on a regular basis, some sporadically) such as *Booklist* (American Library Association), *Library Media Connection* (Linworth Publishing, Inc.), *Library Journal* (Reed Business), and *School Library Journal* (Reed Business). An additional tool that is valuable for the selection and evaluation of geographic materials is *A Geographical Bibliography for American Libraries* (Association of American Geographers). This aid contains a section, For School Libraries, which recommends titles for elementary and secondary schools. Each entry is annotated, and a useful index provides access to authors, short titles, and subjects.

Basic Sources

CURRENT WORLD ATLASES

Current atlases are required for up-to-date information on geographical and political changes in the world. Many students find print versions of atlases enjoyable as well as useful. Probably the most notable single-volume world atlas (print format) is the *Times Atlas of the World* (Random House). *The Times Atlas of the World* is divided into three basic sections: an introduction with general physical information; the atlas proper with a series of regional maps; and a final index-gazetteer section. *The New York Times Atlas* (Random House, print format) is a smaller version of the *Times Atlas of the World*. It offers well-balanced coverage of the world, and because it is moderately priced, it is a good choice for school library media centers. The medium-sized atlas, *Hammond's Atlas of the World* (Hammond Inc., print format) is also appropriate for school populations. This atlas contains numerous pages of maps and provides relative balance to the nations of the globe. *Hammond's Atlas of the World* includes thematic maps illustrating global relationships, as well as several text sections on such topics as the environment and the development of cartography. Another medium-sized current atlas suitable for school library media centers is the *National Geographic Atlas* (National Geographic Society, print format). This atlas contains excellent thematic maps, graphics, and vivid comparisons between places of the world. *Goode's World Atlas* (Rand McNally), a desk-size atlas in print format, is reasonably priced and easy to use. This atlas is often found in library media centers.

Goode's is revised every other year and contains a serviceable index with nearly 40,000 entries.

Rand McNally's America: Family United States Atlas (Rand McNally, CD-ROM format) is a true multimedia atlas, offering sound, pictures, and text, as well as a complete summary of American demographic information. *The Picture Atlas of the World* (National Geographic Society, CD-ROM format) is published by the National Geographic Society. This CD-ROM atlas includes hundreds of maps, photographs, and video clips. Each country has its own maps with text available about vital statistics and background history. *The Small Blue Planet* (Now What Software, CD-ROM format) atlas consists of three primary parts: standard maps, satellite images, and a world political map with historical and statistical data. This atlas is user-friendly and developed with the young adult in mind. *Encarta Interactive World Atlas* by Microsoft Corporation is part of the CD-ROM *Microsoft Reference Suite 2000* and includes many of these features as well.

Numerous online atlases also exist, many of them as a part of other reference sources such as *Grolier's Encyclopedia* (Scholastic Library Publishing) (http://publishing.grolier.com/). Two additional examples of online atlases are *The Map Machine Atlas*, (http://plasma.nationalgeographic.com/mapmachine/) and *The Lonely Planet* (www.lonelyplanet.com).

HISTORICAL ATLASES

Historical atlases are necessary for the study of early exploration, boundary changes, and military campaigns. *The Historical Atlas of the 20th Century*, an online source (www.erols.com/mwhite28/20centry.htm) charts socio-economic trends, systems of government, cities, and wars throughout the 20th century. *The Historical Atlas of the United States* (National Geographic Society, print format) includes hundreds of maps, photographs, graphs, and words of text. Numerous additional historical atlases are appropriate and useful for library media centers. They vary in content, concentrating on either particular periods in history or specific regions. Examples of historical atlases suitable for school library media centers include: *Atlas of Russian History* (Oxford University Press); *Hammond's American History Atlas* (Hammond Incorporated); *Atlas of Classical History* (Routledge); *Historical Atlas of the American West* (University of Oklahoma Press); *National Geographic Society Historical Atlas of the United States* (National Geographic Society); *The Oxford Illustrated History of the British Monarchy* (Oxford University Press); *Atlas of British History* (Oxford University Press); and the *Atlas of American History* (Checkmark Books).

THEMATIC ATLASES

Thematic atlases emphasize a specific subject or region. They currently represent a new trend in atlas publishing. Although they are considered atlases, many thematic atlases more closely resemble finely illustrated popular histories. *The Atlas of North America* (IDG Books Worldwide) has an unusual blend of traditional maps and satellite imagery. This thematic atlas includes black-and-white, natural-color, and infrared images, as well as geographical information on North America. Further examples of thematic atlases appropriate for school library media centers include: *The West Point Atlas of American Wars* (Henry Holt and Company); *The Pacific War Atlas* (Facts on File); *The Atlas of Endangered Resources* (Checkmark Books); *Atlas of the*

North American Indian (Checkmark Books); *Atlas of the Arab World* (Facts on File); *Atlas of the Bible* (Facts on File); *Atlas of the Holocaust* (William Morrow); *Atlas of the Roman World* (Checkmark Books); *Cultural Atlas of Japan* (Checkmark Books); *Rand McNally's Children's Atlas of World Wildlife* (Rand McNally); and *Cultural Atlas of France* (Checkmark Books).

MAPS

At least 90 percent of the maps published each year originate from government sources. The United States Geological Survey (USGS) is the agency officially responsible for domestic mapping. Of all the USGS series, the topographical maps are the best known and most often used. The maps show in great detail the physical features of an area. School library media centers may request free state indexes and other information for the state by calling 1-800-USA-MAPS. Most municipal governments and regional agencies produce maps for planning and engineering studies; they are typically free or are available at a reasonable reproduction cost. Chambers of Commerce usually have detailed city maps, as well as other information on the city itself; they are excellent resources for library media centers. State Departments of Tourism are also good sources of maps, which can be found online (for instance, the online source for Kentucky is (www.kytourism.com). Many online sites exist for maps of all kinds. It is important to remember, however, that it is sometimes difficult to "get the big picture" on a computer screen. In addition, printing can be a challenge. Nonetheless, these resources are typically free of charge and valuable resources for school library media centers. One large, useful online source is CityNet (www.citynet.com). This site provides access to information on travel, entertainment, and local businesses plus government and community services for all regions of the world. Other examples of online map sources are Maps in the News (http://map.lib.umn.edu/news.phtml) and Maps on Us (www.mapsonus.com/). When evaluating a local map, the following should be considered: Is it truly local? Does it show the area in detail? Is it large-scale? Is it current? Is it appropriate for student use?

GAZETTEERS AND OTHER GEOGRAPHICAL SOURCES

A gazetteer is a list of geographical names and/or physical features. It is a geographical dictionary for finding lists of cities, mountains, rivers, populations, and other features. Almost every atlas includes a gazetteer as an appendix that is used to locate the place-names in that volume. Atlas gazetteers are primarily useful for locating major towns, cities, administrative divisions, and physical features. Gazetteers differ from the index to an atlas in that they are generally more comprehensive. *Webster's New Geographical Dictionary* (Merriam-Webster) provides descriptive information for numerous locations. Its inclusion of maps and lists of administrative divisions for major countries and states within the United States makes it one of the most useful gazetteers available today. *The US Gazetteer*, available online through the Tiger Map Server (http://tiger.census.gov/) is an excellent example of an electronic gazetteer, identifying locations via name, state, or zip code.

Geography has supplementary reference sources that contain information not found in atlases, maps, and gazetteers. A geographic encyclopedia, such as *The Longman Dictionary of Geography* (Addison Wesley Longman), is a useful resource, incorporating physical and human geography terms. Current street and road maps and atlases are also valuable materials for library media centers. Both print (such as road atlas: US, Canada, Mexico) and electronic formats are helpful for ready-reference and research-type requests. *The Rand McNally Trip Maker* is a street map in CD-ROM format that is particularly valuable for school situations. Using this map, a student can type in a point of origin and point of destination; the route is then drawn on the map. For each community there exists a fine breakdown of streets and major sites. This resource is moderately priced and updated for a nominal cost each year. *MapQuest* (www.mapquest.com/) is an example of an online street map that enables one to find a specific location and obtain driving directions or plan a trip to that destination. Further examples of electronic street or road maps include *Lycos Road Map* (www.lycos.com/roadmap.html) and *Microsoft Expedia Maps* (http://maps.expedia.com/OverView.asp).

Travel guidebooks are also purposeful geographical resources for school library media centers. These sources deal with down-to-earth facts about specific locations. The most notable publishers of travel guidebooks include Frommer, Fodor, Fielding, and Dorling Kindersley.

As stimulating as geographic materials are for the imaginative mind, they are also an invaluable part of any school library media center reference collection. As a school library media specialist, you will find that there are as many reasons for consulting geographic resources, as there are students in your school. With the introduction of electronic maps and atlases, reference work involving geographic materials is both an exciting and challenging part of reference sources and services for school library media specialists.

Additional Online Geographical Resources

General Geographical Sources

Country at a Glance
> http://www.un.org/Pubs/CyberSchoolBus/infonation/e_glance.htm
> *United Nations data including flag, latitude and longitude, area, population, population density, capital city, languages, largest city, currency, UN membership date, GDP, and GDP per capita. The companion site,* Infonation, *allows one to view and compare statistical data for the Member States of the United Nations.*
> *scope: international*
> *publisher: United Nations Publications*

How Far Is It?
> http://www.indo.com/distance
> *As the crow flies distances between two places. Data from the U.S. Census and supplementary sources; provides a map using the Xerox PARC Map Server.*
> *scope: international*
> *publisher: Bali Online*

continues

World Climate: Weather, Rainfall, and Temperature Data
> http://www.worldclimate.com
> *Historical weather data, providing monthly mean average over a range of years.*
> *scope: more than 85,000 records*
> *publisher: Robert Hoare, Buttle and Tuttle Ltd.*

The World Factbook 2001
> http://www.odci.gov/cia/publications/factbook/index.html
> *Online edition of* The World Factbook 2001, *compiled by the CIA for the US Government. Country profiles cover geography, people, government, economy, communications, transportation, military and transnational issues.*
> *scope: international, current as of January 2004*
> *publisher: Central Intelligence Agency*

World Flag Database
> http://www.flags.ndirect.co.uk
> *Descriptions and illustrations of flags for countries, territories, sub-national regions, and international organizations. Includes national and state flags, ensigns, and sub-national flags. The Flag Institute created the original graphics.*
> *scope: more than 260 entries covering hundreds of flags*
> *publisher: The World Flag Database and Graham Bartram*

Yearbook of International Co-operation on Environment and Development
> www.ngo.grida.no/ggynett
> *Combines independent analysis with reference material covering international agreements, intergovernmental organizations, international non-governmental organizations, and country profiles. Based on the* Yearbook of International Co-operation on Environment and Development 2001-2002, *Earthscan Publications.*
> *scope: international*
> *publisher: The Fridtjof Nansen Institute*

GAZETTEERS

GEOnet Names Server
> http://earth-info.nga.mil/gns/html/index.html
> *The US National Imagery and Mapping Agency's (NIMA) database of foreign geographic feature names as approved by the U.S. Board on Geographic Names. Provides latitude, longitude, area, UTM and JOG number. Note, you must know the country in which the feature is located.*
> *scope: 3.5 million entries; worldwide excluding the United States and Antarctica*
> *publisher: National Imagery and Mapping Agency*

continues

Getty Thesaurus of Geographic Names

http://www.getty.edu/research/conducting_research/vocabularies/tgn/index.html

A structured vocabulary with an emphasis on art and architecture, covering continents, nations, historical places, and physical features. Each record includes geographic coordinates, notes, sources for the data, and the role of the place (e.g., inhabited place, state capital). Names can include the vernacular, English, other languages, historical names, natural order, and inverted order.

scope: around 1 million entries; current and historical; international

publisher: Getty Research Institute

Place Names on the Internet

http://www.asu.edu/lib/hayden/govdocs/maps/geogname.htm

Portal to place name servers; arranged in World, Country, and Planetary sections.

scope: Portal

publisher: Arizona State University Libraries

ATLASES AND MAPS

Atlapedia Online

http://www.atlapedia.com

Physical and political maps, facts, and statistics on countries of the world. Material in the Countries section is detailed, but is undated and unattributed.

scope: world

publisher: Latimer Clarke Corporation Pty Ltd.

Atlas of World Civilizations

http://www.wsu.edu:8080/%7Edee/ATLASES.HTM

Portal for historical atlases and map resources: Greece; Hebrews, Judea, Israel; India; Italian Renaissance; Japan; Rome.

scope: Portal; historical

publisher: Richard Hooker, Washington State University

Peakware World Relief Maps

http://www.peakware.com/encyclopedia/zoom.htm

3D interactive relief maps of continents, mountain ranges, and specific peaks. Part of the Peakware World Mountain Encyclopedia, *which includes photographs, live Web cams, and summit logs.*

scope: world

publisher: Peakware

World Time Zone Map

http://aa.usno.navy.mil/faq/docs/world_tzones.html

H.M. Nautical Almanac Office map of standard time zones, corrected to April 2001, with legend for universal time.

scope: world

publisher: U.S. Naval Observatory

Webliography

CityNet
> www.citynet.com
> *This Web site provides access to travel information, as well as entertainment, local businesses, government, and community services for all regions of the world.*

Grolier's Encyclopedia
> http://publishing.grolier.com
> Grolier's Encyclopedia *includes an extremely useful atlas for schools.*

The Historical Atlas of the 20th Century
> www.erols.com/mwhite28/20century.htm
> *This online atlas charts socio-economic trends, systems of government, cities, and wars throughout the 20th Century.*

Kentucky Tourism Map
> www.kytourism.com
> *This Web site provides geographical information for the state of Kentucky.*

The Lonely Planet
> www.lonelyplanet.com
> *The Lonely Planet is one of the favorite atlases for K-12 students!*

Lycos Road Map
> www.lycos.com/roadmap.html
> *This online map contains many interesting sidelines, in addition to directions.*

Map Machine Atlas
> http://plasma.nationalgeographic.com/mapmachine
> Map Machine Atlas *is a universally known and recommended online atlas.*

MapQuest
> www.mapquest.com
> *This is an online street map that enables one to find a specific location and obtain driving directions or plan a trip to a specific destination.*

Maps in the News
> http://map.lib.umn.edu/news.phtml
> *This interesting site includes newsworthy maps such as Afghanistan Region, Pakistan Cyclone, Tornadoes in Oklahoma and Kansas, and much more.*

Maps on Us
> www.mapsonus.com
> *This Web site includes maps, directions, yellow pages, tours, and so forth.*

Microsoft Expedia Maps
>
> http://maps.expedia.com/OverView.asp
>
> *This online map provides excellent routes and driving directions.*

National Geographic
>
> www.nationalgeographic.com/maps/index.html
>
> *This useful online site offers "Dynamic Maps," "Atlas Maps," "Flags and Facts," and much more.*

Rand McNally's
>
> www.randmcnally.com
>
> *This Web site is a valuable source for planning trips, exploring maps, and finding addresses and driving lessons.*

The U.S. Gazetteer
>
> http://tiger.census.gov
>
> *This online source is an excellent example of an electronic gazetteer, identifying locations via name, state, or zip code.*

Chapter 8

Indexes and Abstracts; Online Periodical Databases

Introduction

A large majority of indexes are now electronic. Indexes, whether separate guides to periodical articles or part of books, are used to reveal specific portions of information in a larger unit. An index is an analysis of a document, typically by subject. An effective index includes enough access points to allow the user to locate precisely what is needed.

Abstracts are an extension of indexes. They present a brief, objective summary of the content, and serve as an aid in assessing the content of a document. Abstracts provide enough information to give the user an accurate idea about the subject area. They are usually descriptive, as opposed to evaluative. A typical abstract is from 100 to 300 words in length. An effective abstract, by itself, may include more than enough information to answer a ready-reference question. A growing number of publications (databases) are now in full text, either on CD-ROM or online; the text is searchable for incidences of the keywords sought. Electronic formats have numerous advantages, such as rapid search of a number of indexes, the ability to move from citation to abstract to full text, and the availability of more points of access through keywords in the title, text, or a specific periodical.

Evaluation and Selection

Evaluation of Indexes and Abstracts

ACCURACY:
- Check that all major facets of the content in the article are represented by entries in the subject index.
- All authors affiliated with the indexed item should be included in the author index.
- Author names should be spelled identically in both the index and the work itself.
- Subjects should represent the content of the publication.
- Effective abstracts should depict an accurate summary of the original article's content.

AUTHORITY:
- Remember that authority primarily relies on the reputation of the publisher or sponsoring agency; three prominent publishers include: EBSCO, H. W. Wilson, and University Microfilms International (UMI).
- For electronic resources, the authority should be verified by talking to subject experts and reading appropriate reviews.
- The publisher or vender should supply the necessary documentation, frequent updates, and information regarding current changes.

FORMAT:
- When evaluating electronic sources, it is essential to consider both ease of searching and standardized procedures throughout all of the vendor's or publisher's indexes.
- Readability of entries is essential for both print and electronic formats.
- Consider the size of type, use of abbreviations and symbols, and font style.

SCOPE:
- An index should adequately cover the materials in the field of interest.
- Consider the frequency of the publication, cumulations, number of subjects covered, and the types of materials indexed.
- Be aware of possible duplications and overlaps in information.

Indexes and abstracts should be evaluated and selected such that they best reveal the contents of the collection, or will refer students to appropriate information not found in the school library media center. Evaluation of print or electronic indexes and abstracts follows much of the same rules as other reference sources. The basic difference lies in the ease of retrieval of data. The following criteria should be used when evaluating indexes and abstracts: accuracy, authority, format, and scope.

A misleading index or inaccurate abstract can cause a multitude of problems. Accuracy is an essential factor in evaluating these resources. It should be ascertained that all major facets of the content in the article are represented by entries in the subject index, and that all authors affiliated with the indexed item are included in the author index. Additionally, author names should be spelled the same way in both the index and the work itself. Subjects should represent the content of the publication, and cross-references should be included as needed. Effective abstracts depict an accurate summary of the original article's content, written by the author of the article or by a third party (for example, the abstract's publishing staff).

The authority of indexes and abstracts relies on the reputation of the publisher or sponsoring agency. Four prominent publishers of indexes are EBSCO, H. W. Wilson, ProQuest, and University Microfilms International (UMI). As more electronic indexes appear, additional publishers will emerge; talking to subject experts and reading appropriate reviews should verify their reputation. It is also important with electronic resources to consider the reputation of the vendor and the producer of the CD-ROM product (which may not be the same as the publisher). The publisher or vendor should supply the necessary documentation, frequent updates, and information regarding current changes.

A large majority of indexes and abstracts now exist in electronic format. In evaluating these resources it is essential to consider both ease of searching and standardized procedures throughout the entire vendor's or publisher's indexes (either on CD-ROM or online). Because some databases do not cover material before the mid-1960s, printed versions may be required for searching older literature. Readability of entries is also essential for both print and electronic formats. The size of type, use of abbreviations and symbols, and the use of boldface type should be appropriate and effective. Arrangement is another consideration when evaluating indexes and abstracts, although, with electronic sources, the search engine will normally reveal the location of a term regardless of its location.

The scope of indexes and abstracts should be discovered. Does the index or abstract adequately cover the materials in the field of interest? Frequency of publication and cumulation should also be taken into account. Typically, however, electronic indexes and abstracts are automatically cumulated. Other considerations are the number of subjects covered and the types of materials indexed. Indexes and abstracts differ in the number of publications included and the depth of the index provided. Some of these sources are quite inclusive regarding the types of materials indexed, while others restrict their coverage to particular titles. As there are many indexes available today, be aware of possible duplications and overlaps in information.

The selection of indexes and abstracts for a school library media center depends on the needs of the students and the characteristics of the current library collection. Many standard resources will serve as aids in the selection of indexes and abstracts. Examples are *Guide to Reference Materials for School Media Centers* (Libraries Unlimited) and *Reference Books for Children* (Scarecrow Press). Additionally, review journals such as the following will include information on indexes and abstracts: *Booklist* (American Library Association), *Library Media Connection* (Linworth Publishing, Inc.), *Choice* (American Library Association), *Library Journal* (Reed Publishing), and *School Library Journal* (Reed Publishing). Cost and student needs are the most critical factors when selecting indexes and abstracts. The price of these resources is an important issue due to the fact that they are usually quite expensive. Additionally, a school library media center will typically require relatively few indexes. It is also important to consider whether the index will provide full-text articles. An index is of little use when the library does not have access to the periodicals indexed. Abstracts are typically only helpful for brief facts, ready-reference-type questions. The cost of electronic databases can be difficult to understand. Different publishers and vendors vary in their pricing options. Licensing is a factor in determining cost as well. Vendors and publishers differ in their approaches as to how much a library media center is charged, depending on the number of users and how they are using the system. The indexes and abstracts purchased should reflect the types of information the students need access to and the student demand for information. General periodical and newspaper indexes are normally required in library media centers. Currently, with the availability of online indexes and abstracts, access to numerous additional indexes is possible without specific subscriptions. In addition, many school library media centers now have online indexes and abstracts available through library consortia, such as statewide library networks.

Basic Sources

The focus of these resources is current, well-known indexes and abstracts appropriate for school library media center situations. These sources provide the access to higher quality information (than a typical Web search, for instance). They are divided into two categories: online periodical indexes, and specialized indexes. As there are countless indexes and abstracts available today, the following are merely *examples*. The following series, ProQuest, SIRS, EBSCO, NewsBank, and H. W. Wilson databases, are fee-based services.

ONLINE PERIODICAL INDEXES

One popular publisher of indexes is University Microfilms International (UMI); their most well-known indexes are the ProQuest series. These indexes are offered online (http://www.il.proquest.com/proquest), on CD-ROM, and in microform. The ProQuest collection online is a Web-based service that allows users to quickly and easily locate magazines, newspapers, and topical reference information. It is delivered in abstract and full-text. The following are examples of the ProQuest collection. *ProQuest Kid-Quest* provides access to more than 100 periodicals, many of them full-text. Charts, photos, drawings, and other graphics are included. This kid-friendly index emphasizes nature, science, and educational topics. Students can select from broad topic areas, such as Health, Sports, People, Plants and Animals, Cultural Issues, etc. *ProQuest KidQuest* also includes the Reference Module, which features the *World Book Encyclopedia*, *CIA Fact Book*, *Occupational Outlook Handbook*, and *Ethnic Cultures of America*. *ProQuest JuniorQuest* includes access to more than 100 core periodicals (90 percent full-text) targeted for middle school research. This index also provides full-text newspaper coverage, charts, graphs, photos and other graphics, as well as the previously mentioned Reference Module. *ProQuest Bronze*, *Silver*, *Gold*, and *Platinum* all offer coverage on popular journal titles (*Bronze* having the least; *Platinum* having the most—more than 2,000 periodicals), full-text coverage of numerous newspapers, daily updates and cumulative material that provide up-to-the-minute reports; the Reference Module is also included. The ProQuest interface allows students to search single or multiple databases, provides integrated subject lists, includes flexible search options, and offers a user-friendly version designed specifically for K-12 students.

The Social Issues Resource Series (SIRS Mandarin, Inc.) (via Proquest; www.sirs.com/schools.htm) is an online resource that provides integrated access to thousands of full-text articles from magazines, scholarly journals, newspapers, government documents, etc. The databases can be searched either simultaneously or individually. SIRS also provides *Research Strategy Worksheets,* which review searching strategies and Boolean operators. SIRS offers four different indexes: *SIRS Discoverer, SIRS Researcher, SIRS Government Reporter,* and *SIRS Renaissance* (*SIRS Knowledge Source* contains *Researcher, Government Reporter, Renaissance, WebSelect, Interactive Citizenship,* and *WebFind*). The *Discoverer* comes in three editions: elementary, middle, and deluxe. It is an interactive database because it includes elementary and middle school curriculum topics; it can easily be integrated into classroom activities. This index strengthens research skills and is developed with the young researcher in mind. *Discoverer* also includes elementary and middle school education workbooks and a comprehensive Educator's guide. The *Researcher* is a general reference database that contains thousands of full-text articles covering such areas as social, scientific, health, historic, economic, business, political, and global issues. The articles are selected from more than 1,000 domestic and international newspapers, magazines, journals, and government publications; they are archived from 1989 to present. The *Government Reporter* contains thousands of full-text articles pertaining to health, science, economics, environment, politics, foreign affairs, business and industry; both current and historical. The almanac databases are valuable tools for researching current and historic government documents, United States Supreme Court decisions, elected leaders, etc. The *Renaissance* includes current, dynamic information on music, literature, film, performing arts, culture, architecture, religion, and visual arts. Many of the articles are accompanied by full-color graphics; it is an excellent resource for both in-depth reports and browsing.

EBSCO is another leading publisher of indexes and abstracts (www-us.ebsco.com/home/school.htm). *EBSCO Primary and Elementary Searchasaurus* (online and CD-ROM formats) is appropriate for elementary age students; it indexes more than 50 magazines of interest to this age level. Through this index, the student may choose Primary or Elementary, Middle Search Plus, Encyclopedia of Animals, and a General Encyclopedia. It can be searched by word or by subjects, such as Literature, Sports, Nature, and numerous other areas. *EBSCO Middle Search Plus Searchasaurus* (online and CD-ROM formats) indexes more than 200 magazines of interest to middle school students; 100 of them are full-text. It is updated weekly; access to data is obtained in the same manner as *Primary Searchasaurus. EBSCO Topic Search* (online and CD-ROM formats) is appropriate for middle and high school students. This index includes 40,000 full-text documents from more than 70,000 sources. *EBSCOhost Masterfile Elite* (online) indexes and abstracts nearly 3,000 magazines and newspapers; 1,000 are full-text. Two other indexes include *MAS FullTEXT Ultra,* which provides full-text for more than 500 magazines and *MasterFILE Premier,* which includes full-text for 2,000 periodicals, covering numerous subject areas.

NewsBank is yet another popular indexing series (www.newsbank.com/schools/). *NewsBank SchoolMate* is appropriate for elementary and middle school students. This index includes more than 500 newspapers and 30 magazines. *SchoolMate* for elementary students is suitable for grade two and up. This database is updated daily and has colorful icons and easy-to-understand vocabulary. The articles selected are from newspapers and magazines of interest to young readers; it includes lesson plans and student projects. *SchoolMate* for middle school students is a cross-curricular database covering numerous subject areas. It includes articles from more than 500 local, regional, and national newspapers, and 30 magazines with a broad range of reading levels. *SchoolMate* is retrospective from 1992 to present and offers flexible search options. *Curriculum Resource* by NewsBank is an integrated, cross-curricular database that supports many areas of study. The information is selected specifically for its instructional value and curricular relevance. This index is appropriate for high school students and adults.

Finally, H. W. Wilson (www.oclc.org/firstsearch) is also a leading publisher of indexes and abstracts. *ArticleFirst* includes items listed on the table of contents pages of journals. It describes one article, news story, letter, or other item from a journal in each record. *ArticleFirst* also provides a list of libraries that have the journal title for most items. Examples of subject areas are business, humanities, medicine, popular culture, science, social science, technology, and so forth. This online resource includes more than 15 million records, is available from 1990 to present, and is updated daily. *Wilson Select Plus* offers both abstracts and full-text articles. Examples of subject areas are accounting, art, education, human resources, environment, and so on. *Wilson Select Plus* includes 788,000 records, provides information from 1994 to present, and is updated weekly.

SPECIALIZED INDEXES

As with general indexes and abstracts, there exist a multitude of specialized indexes covering a wide range of subjects. The following are examples of specialized indexes appropriate for school library media centers:

The Educational Resources Information Center (ERIC) is a federally-funded national information system that provides a variety of services and products on a broad range of education-related issues. It is the world's largest source of educational information and contains more than one million abstracts of documents and journal articles on educational research and practice (updated Sept. 1, 2004). This online database (http://eric.ed.gov) is updated monthly; the information is timely and accurate. ERIC may be consulted for both original and secondary material on education. The system includes: 1) an index to unpublished reports (*Resources in Education*) and an index to journals (*Current Index to Journals in Education* or CIJE, which indexes approximately 800 periodicals in education); 2) an ongoing subject vocabulary represented in the frequently updated Thesaurus of ERIC Descriptors; and 3) a decentralized organizational structure for acquiring and processing the documents that are indexed and abstracted (this resource is moving to full-text).

Resources in Education lists unpublished reports and associated items. Each entry has a narrative abstract of approximately 200 words; authors write the abstracts. Nearly 15,000 items are included and indexed each year in *Resources in Education*. The reports are divided nearly equally among three categories: research and technical reports; proceedings, dissertations, preprints, and papers printed at a conference; and curriculum guides, educational legislation, and lesson plans prepared for the classroom.

Numerous additional online sources provide guides to newspapers and magazines. Examples of these are as follows. *AJR News Link* (American Journalism Review) located at (http://ajr.newslink.org/). This source contains comprehensive links to newspaper and magazine publications on the Internet around the world. Newspapers published in the United States are arranged by state. *AJR* also contains links to radio and television resources in the United States and non-U.S. countries. Another online source is located at the *Internet Public Library* (www.ipl.org/reading/serials). Such resources as Online Newspapers, Online Serials, News and Newspapers Online, My Virtual Reference Desk—My Virtual Newspaper, the *Los Angeles Times*, and the *New York Times* can be accessed through this Web site. *Newspapers Online* (www.newspapers.com/) is yet another valuable source that includes free access to the top 100 worldwide and local newspapers.

The Children's Magazine Guide (print format) is a useful index for children ages eight to 12. This resource includes approximately 50 popular children's magazines, providing articles on sports, science, popular culture, and current events. *Children's Magazine Guide* provides nine monthly issues and an annual cumulation.

ERIC is an excellent point to begin to discover a subject, as some subjects are not found elsewhere. The reports are usually complete with bibliographies, readings, and suggestions for further research.

H. W. Wilson Company offers more than 40 full-texts, abstract, and index databases in print, over the Internet, and on CD-ROM. *The Education Indexes* includes full-text articles from January 1996; it covers approximately 500 periodicals, monographs, and yearbooks. Examples of other indexes provided by H. W. Wilson are: Social Sciences, Art, Essay and General Literature, Humanities, Library Literature, and Information Science and Book Review Digest. This database indexes approximately 70,000 stories; thousands are offered online in full-text. Access points are provided via author, title, or subject for stories from collections; author and title access for stories from periodicals. Subject access includes theme, locale, narrative technique, and genre. Another useful resource, the *Short Story Index* (H. W. Wilson) is available in print, CD-ROM, and online formats and lists stories in both book collections and periodicals.

Two additional indexes of value to school library media centers are *The Federal Resources for Educational Excellence* (http://www.ed.gov/free/index.html) and the *Index to the United States Government Printing Office* (GPO) publications (1976 to present). The GPO (www.gpo.gov/) contains records of items received by libraries from the U.S. Government Printing Office. GPO also includes the Public Affairs Information Service (PAIS), which contains records of articles from more than 1,000 periodicals, as well as thousands of government documents, statistical directories, reports, books, etc. It also contains international materials from the entire spectrum of public and social policy issues. Subject coverage includes business, demographics, education, environment, health, and numerous other areas.

The Columbia Granger's Index to Poetry (Columbia University Press, print and CD-ROM formats) provides an index to more than 70,000 poems and includes a subject index with approximately 4,000 categories. An interesting feature of Granger's is the inclusion of thousands of last lines, which is a valuable tool when searching for quotations.

The *Play Index* (H. W. Wilson, print format) is published at several-year intervals. It includes more than 4,000 individual plays and collections of plays. Of importance to school library media centers, the *Play Index* uses tags, "c" for children through grade six, and "y" for young adults in grades seven through 12.

The average school library media center will typically not require more than one general index due to prohibitive cost and repetition and overlap among indexes. Prior to purchase, review materials should be consulted and discussions with vendors should occur, as well as hands-on experiences with the indexes themselves.

Webliography

American Journalism Review
> http://ajr.newslink.org/
> *This Web site provides news and columns from the American Journalism Review magazine; it is a reputable source.*

Educational Resources Information Center (ERIC)
> http://eric.ed.gov
> *The ERIC database uses the latest search and retrieval methods to cull education literature and provide high-quality access to educators, researchers, and the general public.*

Federal Resources for Educational Excellence
> www.ed.gov/free/index.html
> *This Web source is extremely useful and inclusive, containing such areas as Arts, Educational Technology, Foreign Languages, Physical Education, Language Arts, Science, Mathematics, Social Studies, Vocational Education, and so forth.*

H. W. Wilson FirstSearch
> www.oclc.org/firstsearch
> *FirstSearch is an online service that gives library professionals and end users access to a collection of reference databases. With FirstSearch, materials in a library's collection are highlighted in results from searches in many leading databases.*

Internet Public Library
> www.ipl.org/reading/serials
> *The IPL includes magazines, e-zines, and others on topics such as Arts and Humanities, Education, Reference, and others.*

NewsBank Online Database
> www.newsbank.com/schools
> NewsBank Online Database *is a reputable, user-friendly online source for K-12 students.*

Newspapers Online

       www.newspapers.com/

       This is an inclusive resource that contains everything from USA Search/Map to International Search to Employment.

ProQuest Online Database

       http://www.il.proquest.com/proquest

       ProQuest online information service provides access to thousands of current periodicals and newspapers, many updated daily and containing full-text articles from 1986.

Social Issues Research Series Online Database (via ProQuest)

       www.sirs.com/schools.htm

       SIRS provides a superb online database, aimed toward the K-12 learner.

United States Government Printing Office (GPO)

       www.gpo.gov/

       The U.S. Government Printing Office disseminates official information from all three branches of the federal government.

PART 3

The Art of
Questioning

Chapter *9*

The Reference Interview

Introduction

One of the primary functions as a school library media specialist is to assist students in the use of the library and its collections. As a school library media specialist, you must determine what the students want. This process is referred to as the reference interview; it is an essential part of reference services and a major function of all school library media specialists. The reference interview is fundamentally a conversation between the school library media specialist and the student, for the purpose of clarifying students' needs and aiding in meeting those needs (determining what they want). It is distinguished from general conversation between the school library media specialist and student because it has a specific purpose and structure. In the reference interview, the school library media specialist's goals are to determine efficiently and productively the nature, quantity, and level of information the student requires, as well as the most appropriate format. The effective reference interview takes practice and creativity; this process can efficiently connect knowledge with the students' information needs. It is critical that school library media specialists learn to listen and communicate more effectively with students. As explained in *Information Power,* the school library media specialist "…is a catalyst in generating a spirit of inquiry within the learning community…by promoting careful and precise work at every stage of inquiry, the [school library media specialist] underscores responsible information seeking and use" (AASL and AECT 69).

In discussing the reference interview, it is virtually impossible to divorce human relations from communications skills. It is vital to remember that school library media specialists bring students and information together. It is up to each school library media specialist to ensure that everything possible is done to keep the channels of communication open and flowing. As important as school library media specialists are to students, students are equally as important to school library media specialists, for they are the lifeblood of our profession. Each school library media specialist brings a distinctive personality and unique characteristics to the reference interview process. How these personalities and characteristics, both the school library media specialist's and the student's, affect the interview procedure is crucial. As school library media specialists, interviewing techniques should be refined and interpersonal skills improved on a continual basis. The reference interview bridges the communication gap between the student and the school library media specialist.

In order to properly perform any reference service, the school library media specialist must have an exceptional knowledge of the library media center's collection. Familiarity with resources, both print and nonprint, provides students with accurate and appropriate information. In addition to knowledge of reference materials, the school library media specialist should possess a complete knowledge of the general collection, as well as community resources.

Because questions differ, types of interviews vary also, as well as responses provided (from short and to the point to long and detailed). A successful reference interview is tailored to meet each student's needs. As school library media specialists, the types of interviews that occur most frequently are Ready-Reference, Research Projects, and Readers' Advisory. Each type of interview possesses its own unique qualities; however, all types fundamentally link knowledge with student needs—learning.

Appropriate reference interviews consist of rules, methods, and characteristics that create the accurate connection between information and the needs of students. Reference interviewing is not only an art, but also a science. It can be learned and practiced to produce effective results for students.

The Patron—The Student

One of the most important aspects of the reference process (if not the most important) is attitude—how the student perceives his question will be received. It sets the mood for the entire transaction. It is important that the reference interview is comprehended as a two-way communications system.

It has been observed that the deepest human principle of human nature (young or old) is the desire to be appreciated. By keeping this in mind, work as a reference interviewer will be remarkably easier. As varied as the students' reasons and levels are when asking questions, they have the same basic need—to protect or strengthen their self-concept. The school library media specialist should know as much about the student (social data) as possible in order to conduct the most appropriate and effective reference interview. This is not always easy, nor even possible. However, school library media specialists are in an exclusive position that allows them to gather data about their population prior to interviewing. Nevertheless, during the interview, it may also be necessary to employ substitutes in order to obtain information, verbal and nonverbal cues, as well as other predictive devices, which expectantly discover what the student *wants*.

Each student comes to the reference interview with a distinctive question, as well as an individual personality. There are, however, basic considerations regarding students that are helpful when conducting a reference interview:

- The student may not know what to expect, or the precise reaction the school library media specialist will have to the question.
- The average student may have no pre-knowledge of the type of resource(s) that will answer his or her question.
- The student's communications skills may not be as refined as the school library media specialist's.
- The student may not know the terminology (library lingo) used in the reference interview.
- The student may not specifically know what he or she is searching for, due to lack of knowledge concerning the subject or the particular assignment.
- The student may have a lack of knowledge regarding the library media center (collection) and usage (policies) of the library media center.
- The student may misinterpret the school library media specialist's nonverbal and verbal cues.
- The student may be fearful of the school library media specialist, and certain technologies or frustrated about the question being raised.

As a school library media specialist, remain aware that the reference interview is a two-way communications system. Communications may become *mis*communications when a student is unable to verbalize his or her information need. As described by Kuhlthau, "The bibliographic paradigm is based on certainty and order, whereas [students'] problems are characterized by uncertainty and confusion" (*Inside* 361). The school library media specialist is in the position of fostering communications; discovering, understanding, and mastering the effective art and science of reference interviewing; and connecting knowledge with students' information needs.

The Setting

The physical setting in which the reference interview occurs affects its potential success. The environment of the school library media center conveys a message to the students. School library media specialists have some degree of control over the design and appearance of the library media center, in particular, the reference collection (both print and nonprint) as well as the physical setting. Maximization of comfort and utility are of foremost significance. The following points should be considered with regard to the physical setting of the library as it applies to the reference interview:

- Reference interviews should take place in a relatively quiet, uninterrupted area of the library media center that is comfortable and free of clutter.
- The reference area, the space in which the reference interview is conducted, should contain proper seating and be located near both print and nonprint reference sources.
- Reference materials should be organized in such a manner that the school library media specialist and the student can easily and quickly locate reference sources during and after the reference interview.

The reference interview is a critical component of successful school media librarianship. Reference services begin with an effective and productive interview. The physical setting is a distinct part of the interview, and should be carefully planned in order to provide for optimum communications between the school library media specialist and the student.

You—The School Library Media Specialist

To conduct an appropriate and effective reference interview, specialized skills are required. Some of these skills are tangible—can be taught, practiced, and learned. However, some skills are intangible—your individualism or unique personality. Both tangible and intangible skills combine to create purposeful and interesting communications between the school library media specialist and the student, and hopefully, a successful reference interview.

Each school library media specialist has a badge of individuality that makes he or she unique—the librarian's style. Style, an intangible feature, is a combination of attitudes, appearances, and experiences—a myriad of special characteristics. As indefinable as style is, it plays a significant role in the reference interview. Success, still another intangible feature of the reference interview, is often overlooked as a school library media specialist. Many successful interviews conclude without the student actually finding the necessary information. This may occur because the information does not exist, the school library media center(s) cannot provide the information, or even because the student did not require information in the first place. Regardless, a successful reference interview is one in which the student feels satisfied that the school library media specialist has given personal attention and accurate information.

In addition to the intangible components, there are tangible skills that can be identified and practiced as a school library media specialist: nonverbal and verbal communications and skills. Nonverbal communications assist the school library media specialist in being approachable and interacting positively with students. These skills, in many instances, are already a part of the *style* or demeanor of the school library media specialist. Nonverbal skills are many times the easiest to learn and remember. They consist of the following: physical gestures, posture, facial expressions, tone of voice, and eye contact.

Verbal communications involve what is said as well as what is heard and understood by both the student and the school library media specialist. Verbal skills are often more difficult to isolate and master. Once a verbal skill is learned, it should be reviewed and refined in order to communicate more effectively. Verbal skills essential when conducting the reference interview include the following: positive (respectful) responses, motivational words (encouragers), verbal reflection, positive reactions, avoiding premature answers, diagnoses (or opinions), restating or paraphrasing content, remembering, open questions, and closure. Of primary importance throughout the interviewing procedure is careful listening and response. Talk to the students as if they are important (which they are) and welcomed (which they should be); take all questions seriously. Remember that appearance of attentiveness is also essential for effective communications. In addition, it is crucial that the school library media specialist possesses a genuinely helpful attitude and commitment to growth and the pursuit of knowledge.

Familiarity of the library collection and conducting an appropriate search for information may be thought of as a reference skill separate from the interview. It is, however, a critical step in the procedure and an important part of the reference interview process. Without knowledge of the library media center collection, the interview cannot continue; the question cannot be answered. *Information Power*'s chapter regarding Information Access and Delivery states that the school library media specialist should "...maintain current and in-depth knowledge about the complete range of educational and informational materials..." (AASL and AECT 85). As a school library media specialist, knowledge of the resources—general, reference, and community—creates the context in which the student can ask further questions, as well as locate the desired information. The reference interview process relies on the complete skills of the school library media specialist, including expertise with all the library resources available, to provide the most accurate and complete response, and ultimately, information.

Questions and Questioning

Talk is the very basis of a reference interview, and school library media specialists should deliberately assure that the patron does the majority of talking and a great deal of the deciding of what will be talked about. Genuine listening is hard work and requires that the school library media specialist be alert to all verbal and nonverbal cues that transpire. Interviewing involves the hearing of the way things are being said, the tones used, and the expressions and gestures employed. Defining what is being asked and how to negotiate it is at the heart of the questioning process. Successful questioning requires active listening. This involves paying close attention to all that the student is saying. As a school library media specialist, you must become involved in the communications process; ascertain what the student wants to know.

Three basic purposes of reference interview questioning are as follows:

1) To ascertain what information the student wants.
2) To clarify the question (what it really means).
3) To discover the amount, level, and difficulty of the resources that will answer the question.

These purposes require the school library media specialist to carry on a conversation and to have time for such a dialogue. During the questioning procedure, it is important for the school library media specialist to:

- Determine why the question is being asked.
- Determine the subject of the question.
- Determine what the student has already discovered about the question (prior to asking).
- Determine what information is required to answer the question; the amount and format.
- Determine the barriers involved in answering the question (time, available resources, and so forth).
- Determine the most efficient and effective search strategy.

It is significant to understand that there are two major types of questions, open and closed. Open questions require the student to describe the need and its context. These questions frequently begin with what, where, and how. Open questions encourage further discussion. Closed questions, on the other hand, typically require the student to answer with either-or. These questions usually involve a prior-made judgment by the school library media specialist. Open and closed questions will often intermingle in the course of the reference interview. Once questioning is established, the subsequent search for information proceeds. The school library media specialist should ascertain from the student not only the information desired, but also exactly when the information is needed and in what format. At that point, the reference interview differs from the past, from other types of library situations. As a school library media specialist, it is imperative to foster research and information literacy skills with the student. You should, in most instances, allow the student to conduct the search, locate the information, and to the best of his or her ability—become an independent learner. To paraphrase a portion of *Information Power*'s *Information Literacy Standards for Student Learning*, the information literate student should:

- Access information efficiently and effectively
- Evaluate information critically and completely
- Use information accurately and completely

The successful interviewing techniques performed by the school library media specialist should lead the student to appropriate and accurate resources and foster the student's information literacy skills for socially responsible, lifelong learning.

A successful reference interview, using the most skilled questioning techniques, may not conclude with the complete achievement of the student's information needs (full and precise answer). However, if the student feels satisfied that he or she has been given adequate attention and has been directed to accurate resources, the interview was, indeed, a success.

Types of Reference Interviews

Not only does the school library media specialist need to ask appropriate questions, but must also make efficient use of time. By understanding the basic types of interviews used in school library media centers, this is made more plausible. The three most common types of reference interviews in the school library media center are: Ready-Reference, Research Projects, and Readers' Advisory.

Ready-Reference interviews include questions that can be answered with short and factual information. These questions typically require the use of basic resources such as directories, encyclopedias, almanacs, dictionaries, and handbooks (both print and nonprint). The goal in ready-reference is to provide brief and accurate information in a short period of time.

Research project interviews lie at the other end of the spectrum. These questions involve in-depth coverage of a topic, often requiring the use of multiple sources of information. Research project questions may necessitate several interactions with the student over a period of time to achieve the desired results. As a school library media specialist, your goal is to provide the student with the most adequate materials, then to explain and encourage information literacy skills by the student.

Readers' advisory interviews basically take the form of recommending good leisure reading. As a school library media specialist, you must identify what the student considers good, as well as select the most appropriate materials for him or her. Of course, this is only possible with a current and adequate knowledge of the collection in your library media center, as well as a general knowledge of your school community. When conducting readers' advisory interviews, questions that might be asked of the student include, "What do you enjoy reading?" "What do you not like to read?" "Do you enjoy reading long books or short stories?" "Do you prefer reading a particular genre?" "Do you have a favorite author?" For younger students, showing them a variety of books may be helpful, allowing them time to preview the materials. It is also best to offer several choices. In addition, it is always beneficial, if possible, to provide a brief summary of the book or a booktalk.

Previously described in much literature, as a different type of reference interview, are electronic searches. Electronic searches now intermingle with other types of interviews. Many, if not most, searches will require online information. Therefore, a major goal as a school library media specialist is to locate the appropriate software and technologies, to assist the student with proper searching procedures and techniques. Additionally, it is extremely critical that the school library media specialist assists with proper evaluation of the electronic information. Accuracy and validity of the information retrieved electronically is crucial, still another role in the reference interview process.

Conclusion

The reference interview is an essential role as a school library media specialist. With the advent of new technologies in the school library media center, you are forced into a new pattern of service and a new approach to reference interviewing. However, the basics of reference services and questioning remain unchanged. The reference interview still involves human relations, communications, and interaction with the student. Good judgment and exceptional knowledge of resources remains imperative. The reference interview, in the past, present, and future, connects knowledge with students' information needs.

PART 4

Reference and the Web

Chapter **10**

The Web in Today's Reference Services

Introduction

Essentially every aspect of school library media services has altered over the past few decades due to the emergence of new and innovative technologies. Reference skills, sources, and services are but just one area that has changed to meet the needs of students in the diverse, global society of today. This chapter discusses the Web and how its existence affects many aspects of reference sources and services for school library media specialists. It also illustrates how school library media specialists must work with students to use Web resources to meet instructional needs. The Web, albeit a unique one, is merely one more reference tool for school library media centers.

The day of seeking answers has not ended; only the process has changed. Accessing electronic information has two basic dimensions that distinguish it from print materials. The first is an almost unlimited storage capacity that continually expands. The second aspect is the ability to select from an enormous assemblage of data only what is needed. Mass storage and specific retrieval are both a blessing and a curse. The blessing is evident, but consider the curse. A mass of undifferentiated, many times unreliable information is stored on the Web, which means that there may be thousands—even millions—of citations for any given topic. The problem is finding ways to discover the optimal information from among the heaps of data. As school library media specialists, you now must become the trained magicians who are able to extract (or assist the student in extracting) the desired data to meet specific informational needs. Today, students certainly have access to more information, but this does not necessarily mean that they have more knowledge. Is anyone the wiser because of the availability of limitless information?

The Web offers numerous added avenues and methods of searching. Instead of depending on assigned subject headings, one may use a wide variety of different approaches to gain the needed information. With the availability of the Web, the speed of searching *can* increase. However, speedy and accurate searches are only possible if the school library media specialist (and hence, the student) is knowledgeable about the effective and efficient use of the World Wide Web, including Search Engines. (See figure 10.1: Exercise: search engines, for more in-depth information.)

Figure 10.1: Exercise: Search Engines

Exercise: Search Engines

Search Engines are a searchable database of Internet files collected by a computer program. They allow one to enter keywords relating to the topic and retrieve information about Internet sites containing those keywords. Remember that all search engines have rules for formulating queries; they differ.

To assist you with this, please complete the following exercise.

Ask the following questions as you explore the three search engines listed below:

Does it include links to detailed help?
How large is it?
What type of searching does it use?
How does it search proper names?
Does it have advanced searching?

Dogpile: www.dogpile.com

Ask Jeeves: www.askjeeves.com

Lycos: www.lycos.com

Which one do you like the best? Why?

Which one do you like least? Why?

A Web resource may be different from a print source, but it remains essentially the same in purpose and scope. Web materials *can* make steps easier, considerably more efficient, and certainly more comprehensive. However, it is vital to know when to turn to print resources, when to use the Web, and when to avoid them all in favor of consulting an expert in the field. The bottom line is that correct information must be located for students in the most efficient and effective manner possible.

The Web and Reference Services in School Library Media Centers

The Web is the most important change in electronic information reference services since the development of electronic resources themselves. The greatest contribution of the Internet is not the technology, as impressive as it may be, but the sense of connection it makes possible between individuals and groups. The Internet is not really a source of information, but rather a means of communication—the "ultimate" communication network. With regard to reference services for school library media centers, the World Wide Web is all about providing information. As it grows and continues to change as a forum for the exchange of information, school library media specialists must remain actively involved. As explained in *Information Power*, "Technology is a primary tool used by [school library media specialists] to forge communications between the program and the learning community. Technology…refers to the theory and practice of design, development, utilization, management, and evaluation of processes and resources for learning. Internet links expand national boundaries to allow connection to an ever-broadening circle to enhance students' and others' learning" (AASL and AECT 128, 130). The Web is so vast that knowing what is available is literally impossible; it is growing and developing in many directions simultaneously. The nonhierarchical nature of the Internet can be a challenge and an opportunity for school library media specialists and students. The Internet links thousands of other communication and data networks with one another and with individual users. The lack of standardization, however, requires school library media specialists to invest a great deal of time and energy in learning the variations of most importance to the library and student population. It is a certainty that standardization of terminology and resource formats will become more widespread in the years ahead. As a school library media specialist, you must assist students to effectively and efficiently use the Web, and create information literate students (those who can access, evaluate, organize, and use electronic information) for tomorrow's world. (For further details, see Figure 10.2: Exercise: Search Engines.)

Exercise: Search Engines

Every person searches for information differently and has favorite resources, whether they are print, nonprint, or Web sites. Good searching begins well before one enters the topic terms (keywords) into a search engine. Critical thinking capabilities are as necessary in using a search engine as they are in using any print resource or database. Searching the Web requires part skill, and a little bit of art.

Two useful Web sites dealing with search engines are listed below. Take time to explore them!

1. Search Engine Watch

    www.searchenginewatch.com

    This site provides a wealth of useful information, such as Web Searching Tips, Search Engine Listings, and Search Engine Resources.

2. Search Engines

    http://webreference.com/content/search

    This Web site provides background, how search engines work, and practical examples for getting the best out of them.

As time progresses, there will be numerous potential roles available for school library media specialists—it takes imagination, ingenuity, and much hard work. Success does not come easily. As school library media specialists, we must embrace the continual changes, not resist them. We must move forward to make the school library media centers of tomorrow purposeful and exciting. We must make information gathering effective and efficient—and create information literate, socially responsible lifelong learners. The rewards will be widespread. As the well-known metaphor states, opportunities are like sunrises. If you miss them they are gone. So is the case with technologies in the world of reference sources and services for school library media specialists.

One common *mis*conception is that in the future there will be less dependence on the physical library media center. Why is this concept not true? Information needs are growing and becoming more complex. The result is that that there will be an *increased* need for experts, school library media specialists with skills in searching, accessing, using, and evaluating information efficiently and effectively. In addition, students will now, more than ever before, need to be taught information literacy skills. Who better to teach them than the school library media specialist?

Useful Web Sites

Early Childhood Education Resources on the World Wide Web
> http://webster.comnet.edu/webpicks/weblist/educ_list.htm
> *This site includes such links as The Laboratory School, Child & Family WebGuide, CYFERNET, Parentsoup, KidsClick!, and so on.*

Evaluation of Information Sources
> www.vuw.ac.nz/staff/alastair_smith/evaln/evaln.htm
> *This site offers pointers regarding criteria for evaluating information resources, particularly those on the Internet.*

Evaluating World Wide Web Information
> http://library.queensu.ca/inforef/tutorials/qcat/evalint.htm
> *"Not all sources on the World Wide Web are equally valuable or reliable." This site considers questions to assist in evaluation of Web resources.*

Evaluation of World Wide Web Sites: An Annotated Bibliography
> www.michaellorenzen.com/eric/evaluation.html
> *This site, by Kathleen Schrock, provides an inclusive bibliography of how to evaluate Internet resources.*

Kathy Schrock's Guide for Educators/Reference
> http://school.discovery.com/schrockguide/referenc.html
> *This Web site includes ready-reference and library-related resources; it is extremely inclusive.*

Kids Web
> www.npac.syr.edu/textbook/kidsweb/indexold.html
> *This useful site is "A World Wide Web Digital Library for Schoolkids."*

Reference Materials Collections
> www.cln.org/subjects/refmat.html
> *This Web site offers numerous links related to reference materials; it is divided into "general reference materials" and "specific reference tools."*

Resources for School Librarians
> www.sldirectory.com/libsf/reslibs.html#top
> *This site includes such areas as Learning and Teaching, Information Access, Program Administration, Technology, Education and Employment, Continuing Education, and so forth.*

School Libraries on the Web: A Directory
> www.sldirectory.com
> *This Web site offers a list of library Web pages maintained by K-12 school libraries in the United States, as well as in countries around the world.*

Searching the Internet: Search Engines and Subject Indexes
    www.wldirectory.com/search.html
    This site offers links in areas, such as Internet Portals, Kid Safe Search Sites, All-in-One Search Pages, and much more.

VirtualSalt: World Wide Web Research Tools
    www.virtualsalt.com/serch.htm
    This useful Web site is divided into Search Engines, Directories, and so on.

World Wide School Library
    www.worldwideschool.org/library/catalogs/bysubject-top.html
    This Web site is divided by subject, title, and author; it is an excellent resource.

PART 5

Scenarios and Exercises for School Library Media Specialists

Introduction

It has been said that experience is the best teacher. With that in mind, the following chapter is presented to offer the next best thing, an aid in the form of Reference Scenarios and Exercises.

Three primary categories of reference for school library media specialists are as follows:

1) Readers'/Information Service
2) Selection and Evaluation of Reference Materials
3) User Instruction

Readers'/Information Service involves extremely delicate forms of assistance. As a school library media specialist, you are in the position of crossing a very thin line between reference and readers' service, which accounts for your answering such questions as: What is a good book on 9/11? What is the best novel to read? Will you give me the scariest book you have in the library? Will you find a book about sex education (for a friend)? To complicate matters even further, the school library media specialist is also involved with confidentiality and censorship issues. This all-encompassing area is diverse and complicated, in particular for the school library media specialist.

Selection and Evaluation of Reference Materials is a highly individualized process for the school library media specialist. No two school library media specialists will approach these processes in precisely the same manner. However, one universal, critical rule when considering the selection and evaluation of resources for your media center is knowledge of the needs (both known and anticipated) of your users. In addition, as a school library media specialist, you must consider not only the user (student), but also the community, administration, parents, teachers, and staff with whom you work. It is a complex and extremely significant job.

Unlike User Instruction in public and academic libraries, User Instruction for students is an essential component of the school library media center. School library media specialists do not have the luxury of not providing proper and complete training regarding the basic sources and services of the library media center, including the effective teaching of library skills and information literacy. Indeed, it is time consuming; however, without it little time is available for other services.

In light of these three categories, the following chapter is intended to provide the prospective (or even the experienced) school library media specialist with insight into the numerous situations that may arise in a library media center. The scenarios and exercises are designed to provide the school library media specialist with a glimpse into the world of reference services. This chapter encompasses both large and small library media centers, and urban and rural settings. The situations include both practical and philosophical aspects of reference services for school library media specialists. The scenarios and exercises are to be read thoughtfully, pondered, and hopefully, discussed with other prospective or experienced school library media specialists. The exercises provide useful guidelines for teaching reference skills; they can be accomplished individually or as a group. Following each scenario, a list of questions is supplied for you to consider and reflect upon. As there is no one correct solution for the scenarios, answers are not provided. Expectantly, attentive conversation will arise from the readings, discussions that will search the very heart of reference services for school library media specialists.

Special Notes for Instructors

The following scenarios and exercises are provided as a means of eliciting discussion and spurring thoughtful conversation with and among prospective school library media specialists in the university or college classroom setting. As instructor of the course, your mission is to guide discussion, as well as creative and critical thinking, based on the knowledge, experiences, and insights that you possess. These are simply tools to encourage more in-depth thought regarding specific reference processes and services. They could also be used to guide student discussion in Web-enhanced or Web-based courses. In addition, technologies could be used to encourage the discussions. For instance, students could email other classmates and experienced school library media specialists about the situations and exercises prior to in-class discussions. Adequate, appropriate, and creative discussion will only occur with your expert guidance and direction.

Although some of the questions for each scenario or exercise can be answered with a rather simple response, deeper conversations can occur by providing probing questions. The following are examples of such questions: "Why or why not?" "What if?" "What might happen if?" "Are there alternatives; if so, what are they?" "Can you give another example?" "What ideas can you add to this?" "Why is this significant?" "Do you agree or disagree; why or why not?" "Will you elaborate and explain further?" "What would you do; why?" "What specific documents could be used to assist in this situation or exercise?" "Are there more ways than one to solve this problem; what are they?" "Have you observed this situation actually occurring; how was it handled?" "How might the answer alter due to differences in school setting, administration, student population, and so forth?"

Do not remain confined to merely questions and answers. A variety of teaching methods or strategies can be helpful and valuable using scenarios or case situations. Examples of exercises for use in the classroom include:

- Role play.
- Think-Pair-Share: Provide student thinking time; then, allow discussion with a partner and presentation back to the total class.
- Ask a student at random to summarize another person's point or response.
- Have students describe how they arrived at an answer.
- Play devil's advocate. Ask students to defend their reasoning against different points of view.
- Ask students to create their own questions or scenarios.
- Have students write their responses on paper. Pass these anonymous papers to other classmates and have them respond to each other's answers.

You, as instructor, are the key to eliciting the desired discussions. The scenarios and exercises—and subsequent questions—initiate the process of thinking and planning regarding reference services for school library media centers. You are limited only by your creativity and imagination.

Chapter *11*

Scenarios and Exercises

Scenario (Elementary School): Newsbank

Lafayette elementary school recently received funding from a dedicated parent of a previous student. A large portion of the money was earmarked for the library media center. Mrs. Jean Noe, the school library media specialist, after thoughtful consideration, purchased the online database, *Newsbank,* for her library media center. Jean is very excited about this purchase and realizes how much it can offer her students. However, although she has advertised this new purchase, students and teachers remain loyal to the Internet (for example, Google searches). Mrs. Noe wants to demonstrate to the teachers and students what a useful reference tool *Newsbank* is, but is not certain how to accomplish this task.

Questions:
1) How can an online database be more useful than the Internet?
2) What are the "good aspects" of an online database as opposed to the Internet?
3) List several ways teachers could incorporate the use of an online database into the curriculum. (Try a minimum of two curriculum areas).
4) As a school library media specialist, describe precisely what you would do—step-by-step—to introduce this new purchase and entice students and teachers to us it in place of the Internet (when appropriate).

Exercise (Elementary School): Planning a Search

For this exercise, pretend that you are an elementary-aged student! Then choose one area that interests a K-5 student (I'm sure you have an idea!), such as dinosaurs, airplanes, cooking, drawing, and so forth. Complete the worksheet below. Remember, sometimes when we put things in "black and white," they become more real and you can stay focused (this is something useful to remind your students).

Write down your area of interest and make it into a question.
(For example, how do airplanes fly?)

Go to the school library media center and locate (and read) four reference resources that help you answer the question.
(For example, an online encyclopedia, a WebQuest, a book, and a person.)

Summarize the information you found.
(For example, write one paragraph about what you learned from each source.)

Put the pieces of information together; organize them such that you have a one-page paper that answers your question.

Present your paper in class and obtain feedback from your classmates.

Discuss what you would do differently or the same the next time you needed to conduct research.

Sometimes it is helpful to look at things from the student's side...to provide more helpful references sources and services.

Scenario (Middle School):
Evaluation of Electronic Information

The Glovett Middle School, a wealthy independent school located in the southeastern portion of the United States, is blessed with all of the latest technologies and resources. Mr. Ken Westley has served as the school library media specialist for the past two years; he tries his best to assist all of his patrons effectively and efficiently. Students at Glovett Middle visit the library media center frequently with their classes, as well as independently. Unfortunately, however, the majority of research performed by students appears to be via the Internet.

Ken wants the students and teachers to use a variety of reference tools, but does not know how to accomplish this task. He has numerous reference materials, print and electronic, and would like for all of them to be used appropriately.

Questions:
1) Why are some reference materials more efficient and effective than the Internet?
2) What measures could Ken take to assure the use of all reference sources?
   By teachers?
   By students?
   By administrators?
3) Describe specifically what you would do to employ the use of all types of reference sources. Be specific, taking it step-by-step. (Possibly a strategic plan?)

Exercise (Middle School): Online Databases

The following exercise would be an extremely useful one for middle school students. Think about requiring this next year! Once again, pretend that you are a middle school student. Your school library media specialist (you!) asks you to do the following:

Visit your local school, public, or academic library. It is important to understand that every library purchases specific online indexes and databases. What they buy depends on the size of the library, the type of library, and what the librarian selects (as you know well!). Now, access (from this library) a variety of online databases available. Explore them, go to various links, and learn them (how they work, what they provide, and so forth). *(Remember, just as you learn more about driving a car by doing it rather than reading about it, it is much easier to learn about online indexes and abstracts if one explores and uses them!)*

Answer the following questions regarding the online indexes and databases you explored:

1) What was the primary focus of each online database?

2) What is useful/useless about each online database visited? (Did it contain many pertinent articles? Was it user-friendly?)

3) Can you search by author, title, keyword?

4) Does it include an advanced search?

5) Can you print the information or send it to an email address?

6) On a scale of one to 10, how do you rate each online database?

Scenario (High School): DEAR

The principal at Scribner High School, Joe Rhodes, just announced at the Wednesday faculty meeting that your school will implement a free reading program, Drop Everything and Read (DEAR). Joe also explained that it will begin in three weeks and that Mary Hecc, the school library media specialist, will be in charge of this initiative. Although Mary believes in the concept of DEAR, she is not certain how to obtain buy-in from all of the teachers and make this reading program actually succeed at Scribner High School.

Questions:

1) What is DEAR? (Do your research!)

2) What are the "pros" of having DEAR in a high school?

3) What are the "cons" of implementing DEAR in a high school?

4) What research could you use to show the value of DEAR in a high school?

5) How would you—specifically—advertise and implement this program at Scribner High School. Be specific, using the step-by-step approach.

Exercise (High School): Evaluation of Internet Sites

Not everything in black and white is true! As a school library media specialist, you must relay this information to your students. This (particularly) also applies to the World Wide Web. High school students must learn to evaluate Web sites in order to select reference materials that are valid, reliable, objective, and useful.

Again, pretend that you are a high school student! (This would be a great exercise for high school students to participate in!) For this exercise, view the following Web site and answer the questions listed below.

http://beefnutrition.org

1   Who is the author or creator of this site? Can you contact this person?

2   Is the author or creator qualified to write this work? How do you know? Does the author have any other publications? What are they?

3   What are the purpose, goals, and objectives of this Web site?

4   Why was this site produced?

5   Who published the site?

6   How detailed is the information?

7   Does the author or creator express opinions? If so, are they clearly labeled?

8   Does this Web site include advertising? If so, is that necessarily bad?

9   When was the Web site created? Is it obvious? Has it been updated?

10 What does this site offer that you cannot find elsewhere?

11 How current are the links? Are they useful? Are they easy to navigate?

12 Is there a balance between images and text?

13 Is the site free of spelling and grammatical errors?

Publisher Information

Publisher	Address/Phone/Fax	URL
ABC-CLIO	ABC-CLIO 130 Cremona Drive Santa Barbara, CA 93117 Phone: 1-805-968-1911 Toll Free: 1-800-368-6868 Fax: 1-800-685-9685	http://ABC-clio.com
Addison Wesley	Addison Wesley Longman, Inc. One Jacob Way Reading, MA 01867-3999 Phone: 781.944.3700 Fax: 781.944.9338	http://www.awl.com/corp/
American Library Association	American Library Association 50 East Huron Street Chicago, IL 60611 Toll Free: 1-800-545-2433 Fax: 312.944.2641	http://www.ala.org/
American Psychological Association	American Psychological Association 750 First Street. NE. Washington, D.C. 20002-4242 Phone: 202.336.5500	http://www.apa.org/
Association of Educational Communications and Technology (AECT)	Association of Educational Communications and Technology 1800 N. Stonelake Dr., Suite 2 Bloomington, IN 47404 Phone: 812.335.7675 Fax: 812.335.7678	http://www.aect.org/

continues

Belknap Press	Belknap Press/Harvard University Press Reference Library 79 Barden Treet Cambridge, MA 02138 Toll Free: 1-800-448-2242 Fax: 1-800-962-4983	http://www.hup.harvard.edu/
Britannica	Britannica 310 S. Michigan Ave. Chicago, IL 60604 Toll Free: 1-800-621-3900 Fax: 1-800-344-9624	http://www.eb.com
Brodart	Brodart 500 Arch Street Willamsburg, PA 17705 Intl. Phone: 570.326.2461 Fax: 1-800-999-6799	http://www.brodart.com
Cambridge University Press	Cambridge University Press Edinburgh Building Shaftesbury Road Cambridge CB2 2RU Phone: 44.0.1223.312393 Fax: 44.0.1223.315052	http://www.cup.cam.ac.uk/
Cassell Academic	Cassell Academic Wellington House 125 Strand, London WC2R 0BB Phone: 0171.420.5555 Fax: 0141.240.8531	http://www.cassell.co.uk/
Charles Scribner's Sons	Charles Scribner's Sons University of South Carolina Press 718 Devine St. Columbia, SC 29208 Toll Free: 1-800-768-2500 Fax: 1-800-868-0740	http://www.sc.edu/uscpress/
Checkmark Books	Checkmark Books Facts on File, Inc. 11 Penn Plaza, 15th Floor New York, NY 10001 Toll Free: 1-800-322-8755 Fax: 1-800-678-3633	http://www.checkmark.net/
College Board	The College Board 45 Columbus Avenue New York, NY 10023-6992 Phone: 212.713.8000	http://www.collegeboard.org/

Collier	Collier 919 Third Ave., 14th Floor New York, NY 10022 Phone: 212.508.6000 Fax: 212.508.6160	http://Collier.com
Columbia University Press	Columbia University Press 562 West 113th Street New York, NY 19925 Toll Free: 1-800-944-8648 Fax: 1-800-944-1844	http://www.cc.columbia.edu/cu/cup/
Compton's	Compton's Phone: 617.494.1200 Fax: 617.494.1219	http://www.comptons.com/
Dorling Kindersley	Dorling Kindersley 3 Chandos Place London WC2N 4HS United Kingdom Phone: 44.0.20.7753.7335 Fax: 44.0.20.7969.8027	http://www.dk.com/
EBSCO	EBSCO Division Headquarters Birmingham, AL Phone: 205.991.6600 Fax: 205.995.1518	http://EBSCO.com/home/
Facts on File	Facts on File 11 Penn Plaza, 15th Floor New York, NY Toll Free: 1-800-322-8755 Fax: 1-800-678-3633	http://www.factsonfile.com/
Gale Research Publishing	Gale Research Publishing 835 Penobscot Bldg. 645 Griswold St. Detroit, MI 48226 Toll Free: 1-800-877-GALE Fax: 1-800-414-5043	http://www.gale.com/
Government Printing Office	Government Printing Office P.O. Box 371954 Pittsburgh, PA 15250-7954 Phone: 202.783.3238 Fax: 202.512.2250	http://www.gpo.gov/
Grolier's, Inc.	Grolier's, Inc. 2925 Chemin Cote-de-Liesse Saint-Laurent, Quebec H4N 2X1 Toll Free: 1-800-353-3140	http://www.grolier.com/

continues

H. W. Wilson	H. W. Wilson 950 University Avenue Bronx, NY 10452 Toll Free: 1-800-367-6770 Fax: 1-800-590-1617	http://www.hwwilson.com/
Hammond, Inc.	Hammond Corporation 95 Progress Street Union NJ 07083 Toll Free: 1-800-526-4953	http://www.hammondmap.com/
HarperCollins	HarperCollins Publishers P.O. Box 588 Scranton, PA 18512 Toll Free: 1-800-822-4090	http://www.harpercollins.com/
Hartley Courseware	Hartley Courseware 3451 Dunckel Road, Suite 200 Lansing, MI 48911 Phone: 517.394.8500 Toll Free: 1-800-247-1380 Fax: 517.394.9899	http://www.nol.net/~athel/org/ har.html
Harvard University Press	Harvard University Press 79 Garden Street Cambridge, MA 02138 Toll Free: 1-800-448-2242 Fax: 1-800-962-4983	http://www.hup.harvard.edu/
The Horn Book	The Horn Book, Inc. 56 Roland Street, Suite 200 Boston, MA 02129 Toll Free: 1-800-325-1170 Fax: 617.628.0882	http://www.hbook.com/
Houghton Mifflin	Houghton Mifflin Riverside Publishing 425 Spring Lake Drive Itasca, IL 60143-2079 Toll Free: 1-800-323-9540	http://www.hmco.com/
IDG Books Worldwide	IDG Books Worldwide, Inc. 919 E. Hillsdale Blvd., Suite 400 Foster City, CA 94404-2112 Toll Free: 1-800-762-2974	http://www.idgbooks.com/
Intermedia	Intermedia Information Services, Inc. 13103 Anvil Place Suite 204 Herndon, VA 20171 Phone: 703.478.2277 Fax: 703.478.6656	http://www.i-media.com/

Libraries Unlimited, Inc.	Libraries Unlimited, Inc. P.O. Box 6633 Englewood, CO 80155-6633 Toll Free: 1-800-237-6124 Fax: 303.220.8843	http://www.lu.com/
Linworth Publishing, Inc.	Linworth Publishing, Inc. 480 E. Wilson Bridge Rd, Suite L Worthington, OH 43085 Phone: 614.436.7107 Fax: 614.436.9490	http://www.linworth.com
Little, Brown, and Company	Little, Brown, and Company Brettenham House 4th Floor Phone: 44171.911.8000 Fax: 44171.911.8100	http://www.twbookmark.com/
Merriam Webster	Merriam Webster, Inc. 47 Federal Street P.O. Box 281 Springfield, MA 01102 Phone: 413.734.3134 Fax: 413.731.5979	http://www.m-w.com/
Microsoft Corporation	Microsoft Corporation 5335 Wisconsin Ave. NW, Suite 600 Washington, D.C. 20015 Phone: 202.895.2000 Fax: 202.364.8853	http://www.microsoft corporation.com
Modern Language Association of America	Modern Language Assoc. of American 10 Astor Place New York, NY 10003 Phone: 212.475.9500	http://www.mla.org
Monarch Press	Monarch Press P.O. Box 366 Grass Lane, MI 49240 Phone: 888.283.6767 Fax: 888.517.7377	http://www.monarchpress.com/
National Geographic Society	National Geographic Society P.O. Box 11303 Des Moines, IA 50340 Toll Free: 1-800-437-5521 Fax: 515.362.3345	http://www.national geographic.com

continues

NewsBank	NewsBank 397 Main Street P.O. Box 1130 Chester, VT 05143 Toll Free: 1-800-243-7694	http://NewsBank.com/
Omnigraphics	Omnigraphics, Inc. 615 Griswold Detroit, MI 48226 Toll Free: 1-800-234-1340 Fax: 1-800-875-1340	http://www.omnigraphics.com/
Oryx Press	Oryx Press P.O. Box 33889 Phoenix, AZ 85067-3887 Toll Free: 1-800-279-6799	http://www.oryxpress.com/
Oxford University Press	Oxford University Press 2001 Evans Road Cary, NC 27513 Phone: 919.677.0977	http://www.oup-usa.org/
Prentice-Hall	Prentice-Hall One Lake Street Upper Saddle River, NJ 07458 Phone: 201.236.7156 Toll Free: 1-800-382-3419	http://www.prenhall.com/
Princeton University Press	Princeton University Press 41 William Street Princeton, NJ 08540-5237 Phone: 609.258.4900, Fax: 609.258.6305	http://www.pup.princeton.edu/
ProQuest	Bell & Howell Information and Learning 300 North Zeeb Road PO Box 1346 Ann Arbor, MI 48106-1346 Toll Free: 1-800-521-0600 Phone: 734.761.4700	http://www.ProQuest.com/
R.R. Bowker	121 Chanlon Road New Providence, NJ 07974 Phone: 888-269-5372	http://www.bowker.com/
Rand McNally	Rand McNally 8255 N. Central Park Ave. Skokie, IL 60076 Toll Free: 1-800-275-7263	http://www.randmcnally.com/

Random House	Random House, Inc. 1540 Broadway New York, NY 10036 Phone: 212.782.9000 Fax: 212.302.7985 Toll Free: 1-800-726-0600	http://www.randomhouse.com/
Reed Reference Publishing	Reed Reference Publishing 121 Chanlon Rd. New Providence, NJ 07974 Toll Free: 1-800-521-8110	http://www.reedref.com/
St. James Press	Routledge/St. James Press 7625 Empire Drive Florence, KY 41042 Toll Free: 1-800-634-7064 Fax: 1-800-248-4724	http://www.routledge.com/ stjames/
St. Martins Press	St. Martins Press Oxford Road Manchester UK M13 9NR Phone: 44.0.161.273.5539 Fax: 44.0.161.274.3346	http://www.stmartins.com/
Salem Press	Salem Press Two University Plaza, Suite 121 Hackensack, NJ 07601 Toll Free: 1-800-221-1592 Fax: 201.968.1411	http://www.salempress.com/
Scarecrow Press	Scarecrow Press RLPG 67 Mowat Avenue, Suite 241 Toronto, ON Canada Phone: 416.534.1660 Fax: 416.534.3669	http://www.scarecrowpress.com/
Simon & Schuster	Simon & Schuster 100 Front Street Riverside, NJ 08075 Toll Free: 1-800-331-6531	http://www.simonandschuster.com/
Times Books	Random House, Inc. 1540 Broadway New York, NY 10036 Phone: 212.782.9000 Fax: 212.302.7985 Toll Free: 1-800-726-0600	http://www.randomhouse.com/

continues

University Microfilms Incorporated (UMI)	University Microfilms Incorporated Bell & Howell 300 North Zeeb Road P.O. Box 1346 Ann Arbor, MI 48106-1346 Toll Free: 1-800-521-0600	http://www.umi.com/
William Morrow	William Morrow, an imprint of HarperCollins Publishers Marketing Dept. 1350 Avenue of the Americas New York, NY 10019 Phone: 212.473.1452	http://www.williammorrow.com/
World Book	World Book, Incorporated 233 N. Michigan Ave. Suite 2000 Chicago, IL 60601 Phone: 312.729.5800 Toll Free: 1-800-WORLDBK Fax: 312.729.5600	http://www.worldbook.com/
World Resources Institute	World Resources Institute 10 G Street, NE Suite 800 Washington, DC 20002 Phone: 202.729.7600 Fax: 202.729.7610	http://www.wri.org/

Glossary

The following are simple definitions. They are not meant to replace more thorough definitions that can be located in various other reference sources.

Abridged (dictionary): A dictionary that is selectively compiled; typically based on a larger dictionary (between 130,000 and 265,000 words).

Abstract: An extension of an index that presents a brief, objective summary of the content and serves as an aid in assessing the contents of a document.

Almanac: A resource that provides useful data and statistics related to countries, personalities, events, and subjects.

Authority: The education and experience of the authors, editors, and contributors of a resource, as well as the reputation of the publisher or sponsoring agency.

Bibliographic Control: This term refers to two kinds of access to information: 1) bibliographic (Does the work exist?), and 2) physical (Where can the work be found?).

Bibliographic Database: Machine-readable forms of indexes.

Bibliographic Instruction: Any activity that is designed to teach students how to locate and use information.

Bibliographic Network: Information vendors who provide a centralized database for libraries to catalog, share, and retrieve bibliographic records according to national and international bibliographic standards.

Bibliographic Utilities: (See Bibliographic Network).

Bibliography: A list of materials or resources.

Big6 Information Problem-Solving Model: Developed by Michael Eisenberg and Robert Berkowitz, a process involving six thinking steps one goes through any time there is an information problem to be solved.

Biographical Source: A resource that provides information about people—from facts to pictures of their everyday lives.

CD-ROM: (Compact disc-read-only memory) An optical disc that is an electronic storage medium which is produced and read by means of laser technology. It is capable of containing more than 250,000 pages of information.

Database: Files of information.

Dictionary: A resource containing words usually arranged along with information about their forms, pronunciations, functions, etymologies, meanings, and syntactical and idiomatic uses. A resource that alphabetically lists terms or names important to a particular subject or activity, along with discussion of their meaning and application.

Directory: A list of people or organizations listed in a systematic way; an alphabetical or classified list containing names and addresses.

DVD: (Digital video disc) Videos that are compressed and stored digitally on compact discs for computer access. DVDs are capable of holding up to 20 times as much information as CD-ROMs.

Electronic Database: Files of information that have been computerized.

Electronic Resources: Reference works in machine-readable forms, computerized files of information.

Encyclopedia: A work that contains information on all branches of knowledge or comprehensively treats a particular aspect of knowledge.

Gazetteers: Geographic dictionaries that provide information regarding geographic place-names.

Geographical Source: A resource used fundamentally to answer location questions, such as maps, atlases, and gazetteers.

Handbook: (Also call manual) A resource that serves as a guide to a particular subject.

Index: An analysis of a document, typically by subject.

Information Literacy: The ability to access, comprehend, use, and evaluate information.

Library Catalog: A catalog that lists works located in a given library or libraries.

National Bibliography: A bibliography that lists materials published in a particular country and is often the product of the government.

National Union Catalog (NUC): The United States National Bibliography, which lists all works that are cataloged by the Library of Congress and other members of the system.

OCLC: (Online computer Library Center) A bibliographic network. OCLC has the greatest number of members and links to more than 30,000 libraries in 65 countries.

OPAC: (Online Public Access Catalog) A public catalog (as opposed to system-restricted) that uses search engines.

Ready-Reference Questions: Questions that usually require only a single, typically uncomplicated, straightforward answer.

Reference Interview: A conversation between the school library media specialist and the student for the purpose of clarifying students' needs and aiding in meeting those needs.

Reference Source: A material designed to be consulted for definite items of information rather than to be examined consecutively.

RLIN: (Research Libraries Information Network) A bibliographic network that includes records of the "ivy league" universities and major research centers.

Scope: The purpose of the source and its intended audience; what is covered and in what detail.

Selection Policy: A policy that (ideally) explains the process followed and the priorities established before any resource is purchased and put into the school library media center collection.

Selection Tools: Resources (journals, books, electronic sources) that assist in the proper and efficient selection of materials for the school library media center.

Subject Bibliography: A bibliography that lists materials that relate to a specific topic.

Thesaurus: A specialized dictionary that deals solely with word synonyms and antonyms.

Trade Bibliography: Commercial publications that include the necessary information to select and purchase recently published materials.

Unabridged (dictionary): A dictionary that attempts to include all of the words in the language that are used at the time the dictionary is assembled (more than 265,000 words).

Union Catalog: A catalog that identifies the materials held in more than one library.

Universal Bibliography: Everything published from the beginning through the present (time, territory, subject, language, or form—do not limit it).

Weeding: Selectively deleting irrelevant, out-of-date, unused, and poor quality materials from the school library media center collection.

Yearbook: A resource that presents facts and statistics for a single year.

Works Cited

AASL and AECT. *Information Power: Building Partnerships for Learning*. Chicago: American Library Association, 1998.

Eisenberg, Michael. "Big6 TIPS: Teaching Information Problem Solving: Information Seeking Strategies." *Emergency Librarian* (1997): 25, 22.

Katz, William. *Introduction to Reference Work: Information Sources*. 7th ed. New York: McGraw-Hill, 1997.

Katz, William. 2002 reference missing, see quote on page 57.

Kuhlthau, Carol. "Inside the Search Process: Information Seeking from the User's Perspectives." *Journal of the American Society for Information Science* 42 (1991): 361-371.

Kuhlthau, Carol. "Learning in Digital Libraries: An Information Search Approach." *Library Trends* 45 (1997): 708-725.

Pitts, Judy. "Six Research Lessons from the Other Side." *The Book Report* 11 (1993): 22-24.

Quinn. reference missing, see quote on page 84.

Strayer, Joseph, ed. *The ALA Glossary of Library and Information Science*. Chicago: American Library Association, 1983.

Whittaker, Kenneth. "Towards a Theory for Reference and Information Services." *Journal of Librarianship* 9 (1977): 49-63.

Woolls, Blanche. *The School Library Media Manager*. 2nd ed. Englewood, Colorado: Libraries Unlimited, 1999.

Index